// 5/96)

S0-EIF-069

Real life, real answers.

How to pay for your child's college education

Real life, real answers.

How to pay for your child's college education

by
Chuck Lawliss &
Barry McCarty

Houghton Mifflin Company   Boston

1990

Copyright © 1990 by Lee Simmons Associates Inc.
All rights reserved.

For information about permission to reproduce selections from this book, write to Permissions, Houghton Mifflin Company, 2 Park Street, Boston, Massachusetts 02108.

Library of Congress Catalog Card Number: 89-85918
ISBN: 0-395-51107-0

General editors: Barbara Binswanger, James Charlton, Lee Simmons

Design by Hudson Studio

"Real life, real answers" is a trademark of the John Hancock Mutual Life Insurance Company.

Printed in the United States of America

10 9 8 7 6 5 4 3 2 1

Although this book is designed to provide accurate and authoritative information in regard to the subject matter covered, neither the authors and general editors nor the publisher are engaged in rendering legal, accounting, or other professional service. If legal advice or other expert assistance is required, the services of a competent professional should be sought.

Contents

CHAPTER I

You can send your children to college

Y ou're worried. You dream of your child going to college, but you keep hearing how expensive it is; worse, how expensive it's going to be. Sure, there's financial aid, but how do you get it? And if you do, will it be enough? You know you should be putting some money aside for college each month. But somehow you don't, what with inflation and all. Is your dream going to be just that, a dream?

This book was written to help you make that dream come true. It is filled with the practical information you need. More importantly, it shows you how to put the information to work: how to apply for the various kinds of financial aid, how to cut the cost of going to college, how to save tax dollars while saving for college, how to make your money work hard for you now, and how to get the most for your money when the time for college arrives.

It is true that college is expensive. During the past 10 years the cost of a college education has about doubled. College will get even more expensive. Experts say that over the next 10 years costs will keep climbing at about this same rate.

On the average, it now costs about $10,000 a year to go to college, and a lot more at the big name private schools. Remember the maxim that the biggest purchase you would ever make would be your home? Now your biggest purchase could well be a college education for your children.

However, the situation isn't as bleak as it sounds. The truth is that nearly every qualified student who wants to go to college can go to college. More than half of today's high school graduates go on to some kind of higher education.

This is possible because of financial aid. Aid accounts for nearly 40 cents out of every dollar spent for college. Three out of four college students receive some form of financial aid.

A lot of financial aid comes in the form of low-interest loans. By the time your child goes to college, even more will. The federal government has been cutting back on grants while increasing loans. In this decade, families will pay a greater share of college costs than they did in the 1980's. A heavy burden of debt probably will come with the diploma, especially if your child goes on to graduate school.

There is also a growing number of sources for financial aid. Many states have their own financial aid programs. Major corporations offer aid to the children of their employees. And about one-fifth of all aid is now funded by the colleges themselves. Since 1980, colleges have increased their financial aid from $2 billion to more than $5 billion. Commercial loans are available to students who do not qualify for a government-sponsored loan. There is a surprisingly large number of scholarships available, as you will see.

Another factor working in your favor is that for years colleges had a sellers' market. They could and did choose from an army of baby-boom applicants. Elaborate screening methods were devised to keep out all but the most worthy. Now the number of high school graduates is dropping each year, and this has helped college become more of a buyers' market.

The top colleges still get more applications than they have places for, but many small private schools are hurting. Some

150 small liberal arts colleges shut down in the last decade. More will follow.

Most colleges now try harder to attract students, and financial aid is a powerful attraction. This is why the amount of college financial aid has increased so sharply.

If your child is an exceptional student, the chances of an academic scholarship have never been better. In 1974, 54 percent of all four-year colleges gave non-need-based academic scholarships. Today, 86 percent do. And there is less competition for academic scholarships. The number of students who score 650 or higher on their SATs has dropped almost without exception each year since the early 1960's.

It would be a big mistake to decide you cannot afford to send your child to college, or to not consider a private college. Often the well-endowed private colleges have more resources and greater amounts of aid available to students.

But don't think you can relax and somehow everything will work out. Even if it does, you probably will pay dearly for it. Sending your child to college will involve personal sacrifice. You will surely be required to pay a fair share of the cost. Your child will be required to pay part of the cost, too.

There are also right ways and wrong ways to pay for college. One common mistake is for the student to rely too heavily on outside jobs to make ends meet. At best, this just makes college less enjoyable. At worst, it may make it difficult or impossible to keep up with course loads.

Working while attending college part-time, although admirable, adds a hidden cost—delaying the time when the student can profit from the degree.

To successfully send your child to college you must do four things. One, you must face up to the problem now. If you do, time will work for you. If you procrastinate, it will work against you. Two, you must create a sound financial plan with college in mind, tailoring the plan to your family's resources and needs. Three, you must stick to your plan, altering it as your financial circumstances change. Finally, you must become a canny shopper of both colleges and financial aid. You wouldn't buy a house until you'd shopped around. Buying a college education is no different.

CHAPTER II

Long-range
financial planning

I f your child is a year or two away from college and you have not begun to set any money aside, this chapter is not going to be much help. But don't despair. You will still have access to grants, loans, and perhaps scholarships that will make college possible. Even then, both you and your child may have to go into debt. You may have to settle for a less expensive state or community college. The more aid your child needs, the greater the risk that the college will not be able to provide it. But don't lower your sights until you have to. Don't rule anything out now.

If you do have a few years left before you start writing tuition checks, you still have time to save and invest. Maybe you won't be able to pay all the costs of college out of the money you accumulate, particularly if you have several children. You will still need financial aid to bridge the gap between what you are expected to pay and the total cost of college. But all financial aid is based on the assumption that you have the primary responsibility for meeting college costs to the extent of your ability to pay.

Every dollar you invest now will earn money. Every dollar you borrow later will cost you money. Whatever you can save now will reduce the amount you will have to borrow later. And the less you have to borrow the better.

This book is not going to tell you how to work out a family budget in order to begin a regular program of saving and investing for your important financial goals: a home, college for your children, a comfortable retirement. But if you have not developed a sound spending and saving plan, we urge you to do so, now. You won't get far without one. There are a number of useful books on the subject, including *The easy family budget*, another *Real life, real answers* guide.

Once you have begun a regular savings program you must make decisions about how to invest your money to produce the best possible long-range return. Again, a brief book about paying for your child's college education is not the place to look for comprehensive advice on developing an investment program. You will find some guidelines on the next few pages and some good tips in the next chapter that have specific application in financing a college education. But you should use these tips as part of an overall investment strategy. To develop that, you are going to need a lot of help and advice. You might start with another *Real life, real answers* guide, *How to make basic investment decisions.*

HOW MUCH WILL BE ENOUGH?

Nobody knows what a college education will cost 10 years from now because nobody knows what the inflation rate will be. And nobody knows which investments will perform best during the next decade or two.

But not knowing doesn't mean you should not make some rough calculations and take action now. Certainly, you should have some idea of what you are up against. The chart on page 8 will help. It assumes a constant annual 7 percent increase in college costs for 18 years. It also assumes that right now one year of college costs $10,000. That's a bit lower than the national average, and about half of the total cost of an Ivy League school.

The column on the left shows you what one year of college will cost in one to 18 years. The two other columns show what you would have to invest annually, given two different returns on your money, to accumulate enough to pay for that one college year. For example, if your child will go to college in 12 years, the projected annual cost is $22,522. Beginning now, you would have to invest $933 a year at a constant after-tax return of 12 percent to accumulate $22,522.

And that's only enough for one year of college. To finance four years of college, you would have to invest four times as much each year. Beware: Charts that try to project the future look more reliable than they really are, including this one.

An after-tax return of 12 percent is ambitious and not easily achieved. History suggests that over the long term, the best way to get that high a return is to invest in equities—in other words, the stock market. But the stock market can be risky for short-term investors. If you have only three or four years to accumulate money for college, you should consider a safer investment with a lower return. However, if you have 10 or more years, most financial advisers would recommend investing a substantial percentage of your savings in equities, probably through mutual funds.

GUIDELINES FOR SAVING AND INVESTING

Remember that you need a good family budget and an overall savings and investment plan to get the best long-term results. But these guidelines may help:

First things first

Before you start any investment program, you need a few things in place: life and disability insurance to protect your family if something happens to you, adequate medical insurance, and enough ready cash—at least three to six months' living expenses for emergencies. You also should get down high-interest credit card debt and keep such debt at a low level. Most families should consider making a house their first major investment. Not only has real estate always been a good

A COLLEGE FINANCIAL PLANNER

What 1 Year of College Will Cost: 7% Inflation	Years Until Your Child Enters College	Yearly Investment Required: 8% Return	Yearly Investment Required: 12% Return
$10,700	1	$9,907	$9,554
11,449	2	5,504	5,400
12,250	3	3,773	3,630
13,108	4	2,909	2,743
14,026	5	2,391	2,208
15,007	6	2,046	1,849
16,058	7	1,800	1,592
17,182	8	1,615	1,397
18,385	9	1,472	1,244
19,672	10	1,358	1,121
21,049	11	1,265	1,019
22,522	12	1,187	933
24,098	13	1,121	860
25,785	14	1,065	796
27,590	15	1,016	740
29,522	16	974	691
31,588	17	936	646
33,799	18	903	606

NOTE: This chart assumes that the cost of one year in college today is $10,000 and that the annual inflation of college costs will be 7 percent. The returns shown are after tax.

---

investment, but our government still encourages home owner-ship with a number of tax benefits.

Start early

"The magic of compounding" works its wonders best over a long period of time. Compounding means constantly reinvesting the money your money earns. Want to have a million dollars when you reach 65? At 25, you would have to invest only $103 every month at a 12 percent annual interest rate. At 35 the amount jumps to $328. At 45, $1,097.

Invest with pretax dollars first

Participate in employer savings and investment plans, such as

401(k) plans. Your contribution is made with pretax dollars, reducing your taxable income, and your employer may match some or all of what you put in. The money you put in compounds tax free until withdrawal. You will pay a penalty if you withdraw money from the plan before age $59^1/2$, but you probably can borrow against your money for college expenses. Discuss this with your company's plan administrator. Keep in mind that a comfortable retirement is an important goal, too.

CHAPTER III

Tips on taxes, saving, and investing

S aving and investing for college expenses involves the same general strategies and decisions that are part of any other investment program. That has been especially true since the 1986 Tax Reform Act did away with many of the ways Americans used to save tax dollars. The act sharply curtailed opportunities to reduce taxes on money earmarked for college, but it did not eliminate all of them. There are still a few innovative ways to use various saving and investment vehicles to build up a fund for college expenses.

SAVING TAX DOLLARS BY SHIFTING INCOME

Currently, most effective ways to reduce taxes on money saved for college are based on the same premise: Your income tax rate is substantially higher than your child's. If you are in the 28 percent tax bracket, you must earn $13,890 in order to pay $10,000 toward college costs. But your child, in the 15 percent bracket, would have to earn only $11,765, a difference of $2,125. Shifting income saves tax dollars.

You have two kinds of income to consider, however: earned and unearned (investment) income. Your son or daughter may have earned income of up to $3,000, not pay any income tax, and still be claimed as a dependent on your tax form. The tax situation on income from investments is more complicated. A child under 14 pays no tax on the first $500 of such unearned income. The next $500 is taxed at a 15 percent rate. After that, unearned income is taxed at your rate.

Children 14 and over pay 15 percent up to $17,850 of taxable income, whether earned or unearned. Taxable income is calculated after taking the standard deduction for dependents of $3,000.

Gifts to your child

One way to shift income to a child is by making a gift. You may give your child money, real estate, stocks, bonds—anything capable of being owned and transferred. You can make a gift of up to $10,000 a year (married couples can jointly give $20,000) without paying a federal gift tax. Gifts are not taxable as income to your child. You can't deduct them on your return, of course, but any money earned by the gift will be taxed at your child's rate.

Instead of keeping $10,000 in a bank certificate of deposit earning 10 percent interest, you might make a gift of that $10,000 to your child. Your tax, in the 28 percent bracket, on the $1,000 annual interest would be $280. If your child were under 14, the tax would be $75 (0 percent on the first $500, 15 percent on the second $500), a saving of $205. Compounding that kind of tax saving over a period of years adds up to a significant amount of money.

Or suppose you own a hundred shares of a stock that you bought years ago for $40 a share. The price today is $100, and you'd like to sell it. If you sell it, though, now that capital gains are taxed at the same rate as your earned income,* you would

---

*   Caution: As of this printing, Congress was debating changes in the capital-gains tax rate.

pay a tax of $1,680 (28 percent of the $6,000 the stock has appreciated since you bought it). If you make a gift of the stock to your child, he or she can sell it and pay a tax of only $900 at the 15 percent rate. The stock represents money you had put aside for college expenses anyway, so making the gift and having your child use the proceeds for college is a simple way of picking up an extra $780.

There's a potential problem for families who will be applying for financial aid. When a financial aid analysis is prepared (see Chapters IV and V), a child's assets are not protected to the degree that parental assets are. The less likely it is that you will be applying for financial aid, the more valuable gifts can be.

The Uniform Gifts to Minors Act

A lot of parents get nervous at the idea of a substantial amount of cash under the control of an inexperienced child, who just might decide that a Porsche is more important than Purdue. Years ago the only way to make sure that a competent adult managed a child's assets was to set up a trust. Until 1986 trusts were popular because they could be used to shelter income from taxes. Changes in the tax laws have virtually eliminated those benefits, however. Trusts still have their uses, particularly if a very large sum of money is involved (see below), but you must consult an attorney to set one up.

For most of us, the way to make a gift while still controlling the management of assets is to set up a custodial account under the Uniform Gifts to Minors Act (UGMA) or, depending on which state you live in, its newer sibling, the Uniform Transfer to Minors Act (UTMA). These accounts, which can be set up through a bank or broker, are an inexpensive means of transferring assets to a minor without monitoring by the courts.

There are drawbacks. Under a UGMA, parents are limited to gifts of cash or securities. The assets automatically go to your child when he or she reaches the age of majority, which states define differently as 18, 19, 20, or 21. With a UTMA (approximately 30 states have them), distribution of the assets can be deferred until the child reaches 21 (or 25 in the case of California). Also, a UTMA account allows you to transfer a wider range of property including real estate, royalties, patents, and paintings. There are no restrictions in either kind of account on withdrawing money at any time, as long as it is for the benefit of the minor.

Annual income over $1,000 in a UGMA account is taxed at your rate until your child reaches 14. After that, things get better; income is taxed at your child's rate.

Because of the "kiddie tax," you might want to consider insurance policies that stress tax-deferred growth or mutual funds that stress appreciation of capital in a UGMA account for children under 14. Series EE Savings Bonds and zero coupon municipal bonds should also be considered.

The minors trust

When a substantial amount of money is at stake — at least $50,000 — the expense of setting up a minors trust, also known as a 2503 (c) trust, is more than offset by its advantages. The first $5,000 earned by the trust, no matter what the child's age, is taxed at 15 percent. Also, the trustee, normally a parent, controls the income and principal until the child reaches 21, as with the UTMA. But in a minors trust your child has 30 to 60 days from the time he or she turns 21 to demand the assets from the trust; if the child fails to do so, the trust continues until the time you have specified in the trust agreement.

Shifting income via a family business

You can employ your child in a family business—provided that you pay a salary that represents fair value for the work performed. The business lowers its taxable income by however much is paid, and your child gains an income, the first $3,000 of which is tax free.

USING INSURANCE TO PAY FOR COLLEGE

Life insurance has four important advantages in building a college fund:

- [ ] If you should die before your child is old enough for college, the money from the policy will help pay college expenses.
- [ ] The cash value of a policy is not counted among the assets you must declare in applying for financial aid (see Chapter IV).
- [ ] While the policy is in force, the cash values accumulate on a tax-deferred basis, including dividends.
- [ ] When your child enters college, you can borrow against the cash value of the policy, usually at very favorable interest rates, or surrender accumulated dividends.

Basic whole life insurance protects your family if you die because they will be paid the face amount of the policy. Also, because whole life includes a built-in savings component, the cash value of the policy increases each year as premiums are paid. The insurance company pays interest on that increase. Some companies offer riders that can build up the cash values much sooner than policies without the rider.

Because some plans take time for the cash values to build substantially, whole life insurance is best considered in a long-term program of investing for college. Other types of policies of particular interest include:

Variable life. Cash values will depend on the yield of the investments used in the particular funds you select—stock, bond, or money market funds are the most common. Death benefits can also increase depending on the performance of the investment funds, although you are assured a minimum death benefit (face amount at issue).

Universal life. You can vary the amount of the premium you pay, subject to certain minimum payments. The death benefit also can be reduced and/or premiums increased to speed the buildup of the cash value.

Endowment policies. These allow you to pay up your premiums over a predetermined number of years and choose when you want the face value of the policy paid to you (the spring before your child's freshman year, for example). The death benefit is in effect until the face value is paid.

Single premium life. If your child is going to college soon, you might want to lower the amount of the assets counted in determining your expected contribution by purchasing a single premium life policy. But plan to keep the policy for a while because of the surrender charges assessed within the first few years. Also, recent changes in the tax laws do not make this as advantageous as it once was.

ANNUITIES

A deferred annuity can also be a useful way to accumulate money for college expenses. An annuity is an agreement between you and an insurance company; you pay one or more payments, and the company agrees to pay you a lump sum or periodic payments starting at some future date.

The advantage of an annuity for college funding is that while your money is invested in the annuity, it is growing at a tax-deferred rate; you don't pay taxes on any gain until you cash in the annuity or start receiving payments from the contract. The disadvantage is that under most circumstances, if you cash in the contract before age $59^1/2$, you will have to pay a 10 percent penalty on the *growth* in your investment. Some contracts, however, will permit you to borrow against the annuity; this is to your advantage if you will need the money before you reach age $59^1/2$.

Annuities can be single premium (you pay one lump sum, up front) or annual premium (you make annual payments for a period of time). The contract can be for a fixed annuity, which generally offers a guaranteed minimum rate of return, or for a variable annuity. The return on a variable depends on how well the investments in your annuity performed. For purposes of college financial planning, the fixed annuity may be the better choice.

Annuities are most useful when college expenses are at least 8 to 10 years away, allowing adequate time for tax-deferred growth. You should look carefully at the tax consequences before investing in an annuity, but you may well find it a good choice.

SAVING SPECIFICALLY FOR COLLEGE EXPENSES

With quite a few years to go before you write your first check for college tuition, your best strategy is to build up a diversified portfolio that includes stocks as well as such investments as bonds and money market funds. You have a large number to choose from and books and advisers to turn to for help. Here are a few ideas especially well-suited to funding college expenses:

Series EE U.S. Savings Bonds. Interest on bonds purchased in 1990 or later is tax free for families with incomes under $60,000 (tax reduced for incomes up to $90,000), *if* the bonds are cashed to pay for college expenses. The minimum yield on bonds held for five years is 6 percent. The interest rate will be increased as the average return on five-year Treasury bills increases. The tax-free feature of savings bonds should make their actual yield comparable to those of certificates of deposit and money market funds.

Guaranteed tuition plans. At least three states (Michigan, Florida, and Wyoming) now allow you to pay your child's entire college tuition bill as early as the day after he or she is born. Many other states are considering such plans as of this writing; yours might be one of them. A few colleges are also offering this option.

The state plans allow for a choice among state colleges and sometimes private colleges within the state. You pay at a greatly discounted rate, of course, and the state has the use of your money for the intervening years.

The hitch is that if your child does not go to a school that is part of the plan, you get back your principal, but are likely to lose some or even all of the interest that your money has earned all those years. It is still worth finding out what your state offers, though the provisions of these plans promise to evolve quickly.

State savings plans. Quite a few states now offer tax-free bond investment programs to help parents pay for college. The bonds typically mature from 5 to 20 years after you buy them. Most states do not require attendance at a state school.

Bank savings plans. More and more banks are offering

special college savings plans. One of the earliest and best-known plans is the College Sure CD offered by the College Savings Bank of Princeton, New Jersey (800-342-6670; zip 08540). The bank provides an individualized projection of college costs and investment strategies based on your child's current age and the type of college he or she may wish to attend. There is no charge for this service, even if you choose not to participate in the plan. If you do choose to follow the plan, the yield on your FDIC-insured CD is linked to the average annual increases in tuition, fees, room and board at a composite 500 private and state colleges. Other investments may produce a better return, but if college inflation gets even worse, the guarantee of this CD may look very good.

Certificates of deposit. CDs are a conservative and useful savings vehicle. When you buy one specifically to put money away for college, you can time it to mature a couple of weeks before tuition is due.

Home equity loans. If you use the proceeds to finance a college education, you can deduct the interest on a home equity loan on your tax return. For families whose homes have greatly appreciated in value over the years, such loans are a tempting way to tap the equity they have built up. But keep in mind that there are some stiff fees involved, as well as interest payments. And make sure you have considered the stakes involved when you put your home on the line as collateral.

Zero coupon bonds. These do not offer any special tax breaks just because you use them to pay for a college education, but zero coupon bonds are a useful device for building a college fund. "Zeros" don't pay semiannual interest the way most bonds do. Instead, you buy them at a deeply discounted price and cash them in for their full face value at a set date.

Let's say your child will enter college in 10 years. If you were to buy $10,000 worth of 10-year zero coupon municipal bonds at 7 1/2 percent interest, you would pay just $4,852 for the bonds. In 10 years you would cash them in for $10,000. Because they are municipal bonds, there would be no federal tax liability. If you buy taxable zeros, you have to pay taxes on the interest each year you hold the bonds, even though you don't get the interest annually.

CHAPTER IV

How much is college going to cost?

I n many ways, sending your child to college involves a financial process much like the one you went through when you bought your home. First, you decide what you want and find out how much it costs. Then you determine your financial resources: how large a down payment you can make and how much you can pay a month. The final step is shopping for the mortgage, the financing package that will make your dream come true.

Similarly, the first step in sending your child to college is determining which colleges you like and how much they cost. Then find out how much you and your child will be expected to contribute. Finally, explore ways to make up the difference. However wide the gap between your resources and the cost of college, there are ways of bridging it.

DETERMINING COLLEGE COSTS

During your child's junior year in high school, develop a list of colleges both of you believe would be sound choices. Then become a comparison shopper. Write to the schools and ask for information on costs. Most colleges have brochures that set out their costs and financial aid policies.

Don't be afraid to think big. Remember that prestigious private colleges usually have more college-based aid available for their students. Study the information from the colleges. Then work up the total annual cost of each college, adding expenses pertinent to your son or daughter.

You may be surprised by how much tuition and fees vary from college to college. The biggest difference is between public and private colleges. Private colleges invariably cost more. However, state schools charge more for tuition for out-of-state students, and this may bring the cost up to that of some private schools.

Room and board are the other major expenses. Will your child live in a dormitory, off campus, or live at home while commuting to a nearby college? Remember that this arrangement costs money, too. Where the college is located affects the cost of room and board. Living costs are higher for those attending Columbia in New York City than for those attending Vanderbilt in Nashville.

The location of the school affects the cost in another way. Will your child have to fly to and from college? Add air fare to your list of expenses. Commuting from home? Add in items such as gasoline and automobile repairs. Consider what will happen to your telephone bill if the college is 2,000 miles from home.

Books and supplies are fairly standard expense items from college to college, but the costs do vary depending on your child's field of study. The college should be able to give you an accurate estimate for a particular discipline.

The more your child participates in the social life of the college the more money you should add in to cover clothing, fraternity or sorority dues, and out-of-pocket expenses.

Go over the list one more time to make sure you haven't missed anything. Have you figured in medical costs? Any extra insurance your child might need? Try to itemize all the things that may come up during a typical college year and what they

ESTIMATING STUDENT EXPENSES

	College A	College B	College C
Tuition and fees	$8,900		
Books and supplies	400		
Room	2,300		
Board*	2,100		
Personal **	800		
Transportation ***	650		
TOTALS:	15,150		

* If the student commutes, board should be considered a family expense.
** Clothing, laundry, recreation, medical, telephone, etc.
*** The cost of two or three round trips home, or transportation to and from college If the student lives at home.

may cost.

Now add everything up. Chances are, the figure is larger than you first anticipated. But don't be discouraged. Even families with incomes over $75,000 can get financial assistance.

DETERMINING FAMILY NEED

In order to receive financial aid, you must prove you need it. Most aid available to college students today is based on proven need. Your need is the difference between the cost of college and the amount you and your child will be expected to pay.

A formula, called Congressional Methodology Need Analysis, is used to determine your contribution. In 1986 Congress enacted a law that made use of this formula mandatory to determine what families would have to contribute to be eligible for federal grants, need-based loans, and campus work programs. Your application for financial aid (see Chapter V) will be evaluated by a processing organization using Congressional Methodology.

The formula uses the financial information you submit. It considers a number of factors: family income, assets, your age, marital status, family size, the number of children you have in college, living expenses, and medical expenses, for example.

All the factors are used to come up with an amount called

DETERMINING THE PARENTAL CONTRIBUTION

The sample analysis is based on a family of four with one child applying to college; the father is 50. The worksheets and charts make use of 1989–90 percentages and allowances and are adapted from those prepared by the College Scholarship Service.

Income	Sample	Your family
Father's annual income	$32,000	_____
Mother's annual income	4,000	_____
Other income (interest, dividends, etc.)	1,000	_____
A. Total income	37,000	_____
Expenses:		
Federal and state income taxes	6,800	_____
Social Security taxes (maximum $3,380 per person)	2,704	_____
Medical expenses in excess of 5 percent of total income (including dental and insurance premiums)	1,200	_____
Elementary and high school tuition for dependents (up to $3,750 per child)	0	_____
Employment allowance (If both parents work, 35 percent of lower income; if a single parent household, 35 percent of the income; maximum of $2,130)	1,400	_____
* Standard maintenance allowance	13,740	_____
B. Total allowances	25,844	_____
C. Available income (line A – line B)	11,156	_____
Assets:		
Equity in home (current market value less mortgage)	60,000	_____
Business or farm**	0	_____
Savings	5,500	_____
Investments (current value)	12,500	_____
D. Total assets	78,000	_____
E. Asset protection allowance*	44,300	_____
F. Remaining assets (Line D – line E)	33,700	_____
G. Income supplement from assets**	4,044	_____
H. Adjusted available income (Line C + line G)	15,200	_____
I. Parental contribution***	3,994	_____

*   "Maintenance allowance" is what your family needs to maintain a reasonable standard of living, according to Congressional Methodology (see table below).

**   A percentage of your business or farm net worth is considered an available asset (see table below for appropriate percentage for your calculations).

*** "Asset protection allowance" takes into account the age of the older parent (older parents get to protect more), and whether the student is from a one- or two-parent family (two-parent families get to protect more, see table below).

**** 12 percent of your unprotected assets are considered available to supplement income (see table below).

***** See the table on page 24.

TABLES USED TO COMPUTE ALLOWANCES AND ADJUSTMENTS

Standard maintenance allowance

Family size (including applicant)	Family members in college				
	1	2	3	4	5
2	$8,930	$7,410			
3	11,130	9,600	$8,080		
4	13,740	12,220	10,690	$9,170	
5	16,210	14,690	13,170	11,640	$9,050
6	18,960	17,440	15,920	14,390	12,870

For each additional family member, add $2,140.
For each additional college student, subtract $1,520.

Business or farm adjustments

NET WORTH (NW)	ADJUSTMENT RATE
Less than $1	$0
	$1 – $65,000 40 percent of NW
$65,001 – $190,000	$26,000 + 50 percent of NW over $65,000
$190,001 – $320,000	$88,500 + 60 percent of NW over $190,000
$320,001 or above	$166,500 + 100 percent of NW over $320,000

Asset protection allowance

AGE	TWO-PARENT FAMILY	ONE-PARENT FAMILY
39 or less	$30,200	$22,700
40–44	34,100	25,400
45–49	38,800	28,500
50–54	44,300	32,100
55–59	51,800	36,300
60–64	60,900	41,900
over 65	67,500	45,700

Income supplement from assets when
remaining assets are negative (When remaining assets are $0 or more, use 12%.)

AVAILABLE INCOME	USE:
$ 1,333 or less	6%
1,334 – 4,000	5%
4,001 – 6,667	4%
6,668 – 9,333	3%
9,334 – 12,000	2%
12,001 – 14,667	1%
14,668 or more	0%

your Adjusted Available Income (AAI). Your Adjusted Available Income probably will be considerably less than your taxable income, sometimes less than half. Some needy families have a negative AAI. Then, as the chart indicates, a percentage of your AAI becomes the amount you are expected to contribute.

PARENTAL CONTRIBUTION

The following chart is used to determine the amount of the parental contribution. This contribution is the *total* you will be expected to pay for all college students in your family. To calculate the amount you will be asked to pay for each individual student, divide the amount by the number of family members who are at least half-time college students. Be aware that financial aid officers can use professional judgment regarding special circumstances that may affect the parental contribution.

Expected Parental Contribution

Adjusted Available Income (AAI)			Parental Contribution
Less than		–$3,409	$750
–$3,409	to	$8,000	22% of AAI
$8,001	to	$10,000	$1,760 + 25% of AAI over $8,000
$10,001	to	$12,000	$2,260 + 29% of AAI over $10,000
$12,001	to	$14,100	$2,840 + 34% of AAI over $12,000
$14,100	to	$16,000	$3,554 + 40% of AAI over $14,100
$16,101	to	more	$4,354 + 47% of AAI over $16,100

THE STUDENT'S CONTRIBUTION

Your child must also make a financial contribution to college expenses. This amount is arrived at through another standard formula that considers any assets your child has and the amount of money he or she has earned in the previous year. Keep in mind that the child's assets are assessed at a rate some six times greater than that of the parent's assets (35 percent versus 6 percent).

Real life, real answers.

P eggy Caldwell has been the sole supporter of her three children since her divorce 10 years ago. She earns $22,360 as a bookkeeper. The house awarded to her in the settlement is now worth about $58,000. She has been unable to save any money, and for good reason. She has put one son through the state college, another son is a junior there, and her daughter, Phyllis, is a freshman at a private college.

Peggy's parental contribution is $3,142. Half this amount will go toward her son's college expenses, the other half toward Phyllis's expenses. The expected contribution from Phyllis is $2,288, partly from her summer job as a lifeguard at a resort, the rest from savings. Her financial aid package is made up of grants augmented by student loans and work funds:

College grant	$7,750
Pell grant	1,550
Stafford loan	2,200
Perkins loan	1,200
Work-study (game room monitor)	750
Total aid:	$13,450

INDEPENDENT STUDENT STATUS

An important question on the financial aid application deals with whether your child will be classified as a dependent or independent student. If the student is considered "emancipated," parental income and financial assets will not be a factor in determining financial aid. But you cannot simply declare your child self-supporting and refuse to help with college expenses. The student must meet eligibility criteria such as the following:

☐ Be 24 years old or over.
☐ Be a veteran of the U.S. armed forces.
☐ Be an orphan or ward of the court.
☐ Have a legal dependent and pay at least half its support.

Any one of the above will automatically qualify a student as independent. There are other possibilities. If the student has earned at least $4,000 for the past two years and you have not claimed him or her as a dependent on your last two tax returns, the student may qualify. If the student is married and no longer being claimed as a dependent, the student may qualify, too. In either case, living at home does not automatically make your child your dependent.

The contribution of an independent student is based on only two factors: student (and spouse, if any) income and student (and spouse, if any) assets.

The college financial aid administrator has the authority to reclassify your child an independent student if the circumstances warrant it.

CHAPTER V

How to get financial aid

I n the recent past, practically all colleges admitted students solely on their ability to succeed academically. Operating under a "need-blind" admissions policy, the admissions office was not even aware if a student had applied for financial aid. If the student were admitted and an aid application submitted, the aid decisions then were made, generally to the full extent of the need.

Today some colleges cannot afford a "need-blind" policy, and a few will deny admission to some students with high financial needs. Others have an "admit-deny" policy. The student is admitted but not given financial aid to meet demonstrated need.

Most schools, though, try to make college financially possible for as many students as they can. This is good news for middle- and upper-middle-class families. So don't count yourself out. *Apply!*

The financial aid process is complex, however, and the application itself takes time and careful attention to detail. Let's take an overview of the process.

WHAT TYPES OF AID SHOULD YOU APPLY FOR?

You should be applying for four types of aid: federal, state (if available), institutional, which is arranged by the college the student attends, and private (see Chapter VIII).

It is important to apply for all types of aid even if you think you will not qualify for a particular type, such as a Pell grant. In fact, only about one in five students who apply for a Pell grant will receive one, but most schools require that you apply for one before considering you for any other type of financial award. A great number of students who do not qualify for Pell grants do go on to receive generous state and/or institutional aid, including much in the form of outright scholarship.

Applications for all types of aid undergo the need analysis process described in the previous chapter. This is generally handled by one of two private organizations, the College Scholarship Service (CSS) or American College Testing (ACT).

WHAT APPLICATION FORMS ARE NEEDED?

Look through the application materials that the colleges send you. In the financial aid information, you will find out what forms are required.

For the institutional aid application, most schools use either the Financial Aid Form (FAF), which is processed by CSS, or the Family Financial Statement (FFS), which is handled by ACT. The forms themselves, however, are not always provided by the colleges. The student can pick them up from the guidance office at his or her high school or get them directly from the issuing organizations. Some schools will require a separate institutional application as well. If that is the case, it will be provided by the college.

To apply for federal aid, you may use the free Application for Federal Student Aid (AFSA), available from your high school guidance counselor. If you are using the FAF or FFS, however, federal aid consideration will be based on information you provide on that form.

Some colleges use neither the FFS nor the FAF. They may direct you to use only the free federal AFSA or a state grant application similar to the FAF or FFS (used in Illinois and Pennsylvania).

Real life, real answers.

B ob Smyth, a senior in high school, was starting the college application process with the help of his parents. Both parents worked, but with Bob's two older sisters in college, they knew they would need financial aid. Bob decided to apply to three private colleges and one state university. The deadline for the admissions applications was January 1; financial aid applications were due February 12. Two of the private colleges required the FAF, one used the FFS, and the state school also required its own form. Bob and his parents spent a weekend filling in the three forms. They were relieved that they didn't have to file an AFSA as well; Bob's application for a Pell grant was automatically triggered by both the FAF and FFS.

Bob had just received his pilot's license and was considering applying for an Air Force ROTC scholarship, but ultimately decided against it. He did research other sources of scholarships and applied for a $1,000 scholarship through his father's union.

Eventually Bob heard from the schools. He was admitted to the state school and two of the private colleges; he was rejected at the other private college. He and his parents looked over the financial aid awards and decided that the aid package from one of the private schools made it as affordable as the state school.

Bob had not been deemed eligible for a Pell grant, but the aid package included a $5,000 scholarship from the school itself. Bob would have to take out a $2,500 Stafford loan (the award letter included information on how to apply for it) and have an on-campus job. Bob felt that it was only fair that he assume some of the financial responsibility for his education.

Bob got the $1,000 scholarship from his father's union and notified the school's financial aid office. Essentially, the college split the award with Bob. His loan obligation was reduced by $500, but his scholarship was reduced by $500 as well. His parents' contribution was unchanged.

COVERING YOUR FINANCIAL AID BASES

1. Apply for institutional aid at the colleges to which you have applied for admission. Use the Family Financial Statement (FFS), the Financial Aid Form (FAF), the Application for Federal Student Aid (AFSA), and/or the college's own form—whichever the college requires. Apply for financial aid before you receive admission notification. Deadlines for financial aid applications vary with the colleges.

2. Apply for a Pell grant using the AFSA. If you file an FAF, FFS, or AFSA for institutional aid, your application for a Pell grant will be triggered automatically.

3. Begin researching and applying for private scholarships (see Chapter VIII for suggestions).

4. Decide if the military route to college makes sense for you. Chapter IX offers more information about military opportunities.

5. Apply for a loan after you have formally accepted an offer of admission from a college and after you have seen your financial aid award. The award package will, among other things, detail the type or types of loans for which you should apply. Chapter VII describes the major types of loans.

If your child is applying for aid at several colleges in different parts of the country, you may have to fill out several different applications. This will be time consuming, but since each form asks for basically the same financial information, the process is easier than it appears.

Completing the applications

Your child actually prepares the application, but he or she will need you to fill in the required figures. You must bare your financial soul. Some parents are reluctant to share this information with anyone, even their children. But since paying for college is a joint responsibility of parent and child, a frank discussion of your financial circumstances is in order. Keep in mind that you must be forthright in your financial disclosure if your child is to receive aid.

Applications are not accepted until January 1 of the year the student will attend college; the deadlines will vary, most being a few months later. Keep in mind that some colleges award aid on a first-come, first-served basis. In those cases, the sooner after January 1 the application is made, the better.

The income figures are the same as the ones you will use on your federal income tax form. If you are not going to file promptly, use an estimate and supply the actual figures if required later. In addition, gather your year-end statements from savings and money market accounts, stock or money management portfolios, records of medical expenses, home mortgage, individual retirement programs, etc.

You will need the same information about your child's financial circumstances: income for the year just ended, savings account balance, trust funds, etc.

Now you and your child are ready to complete the applications. If several schools request a need analysis from the same organization, simply indicate to which school (or schools) the results should be sent.

Once the applications are completed, they are sent back to the appropriate processor. CSS and ACT charge a processing fee; the amount varies with the number of schools to which the results are sent. This fee may be waived in cases of true hardship. No fee is charged for the federal grant application (AFSA).

WHAT HAPPENS NEXT?

Using the Congressional Methodology, the need analysis service determines the contribution expected from you and your child. This process takes about four weeks. A report is sent to your child, the colleges, and any financial aid organizations indicated on the application. The student will also be notified of Pell grant eligibility through a Student Aid Report, which eventually should be given to the college the student chooses to attend.

The college financial aid officer then determines whether the student is eligible for financial aid. To be eligible, a student must:

Real life, real answers.

Floyd Nolan was a superintendent in a knitting factory until he retired. His pension and Social Security benefits totaled $17,976 a year. Floyd married late in life, and he and his wife, Cora, who isn't employed, have two children: a daughter, Billie Jean, in her first year of college, and a son just entering high school. The Nolans have $2,700 in a savings account and have paid off the mortgage on their house, which is now worth $75,000.

The college set the Nolans' parental contribution at $734; Billie Jean's at $1,339. Billie Jean works summers in the office of the knitting factory. The total Nolan contribution of $2,073 fell $15,252 short of meeting her college expenses.

The college made up nearly half the difference with a grant. The total aid package for Billie Jean included a job in the college library, four grants, and a loan:

College grant	$7,605
Pell grant	1,550
State grant	2,000
SEOG grant	760
Stafford loan	2,625
Work-study program	900
Total aid:	$15,440

☐ Apply for a course of study leading to a degree or certificate.

☐ Once enrolled, maintain satisfactory academic progress.

☐ Not be in default on an aid loan or in debt on a grant.

☐ Be a U.S. citizen or an eligible noncitizen.

☐ If male and over 18, be registered with Selective Service.

The aid officer then reviews the need analysis report. You may be asked for additional information or to verify the information you submitted. Some colleges ask for financial documentation from all applicants.

If the student's parents are divorced, colleges may handle the situation differently. Some ask for financial disclosures from the noncustodial parent; others do not, relying on the FAF or FFS, which are based only on information supplied by the custodial parent. If the custodial parent has remarried, however, the stepparent's financial status must be included to complete the aid analysis. Should a noncustodial parent be unwilling to provide requested information or contribute toward the college costs, the college will ask for an explanation.

With all the information in hand, the aid officer reviews the contribution expected from you and your child. The figure might be lowered, but it could also be raised. The officer uses his or her professional judgment regarding special circumstances before deciding how much you will have to contribute. The officer then subtracts the family contribution from the college's

Real life, real answers.

F red and Wanda Cohen divorced in 1986 when their only child, Sylvia, was a sophomore in high school. A chemical engineer for a large industrial corporation, Fred earns $52,000 a year and paid child support until Sylvia was 18. Wanda, a receptionist in a law office, earns $20,910, has $5,000 in savings, and owns her $80,000 home. She is the custodial parent, and neither she nor Fred has remarried.

Under the formula used to calculate the parental contribution, Fred did not have to contribute to Sylvia's college education. But the college aid officer, noting Fred's income and lack of family obligations, decided to assess him anyway. Fred agreed to contribute. His contribution was set at $4,142; Wanda's at $2,766. Sylvia had $11,000 in savings, most of it a gift from her father, and from that she was assessed $3,850. Another $877 was assessed from her summer earnings as a clerk in a department store. If Fred had not agreed to contribute, the aid officer probably would have replaced his contribution with student loans.

The three Cohens contributed a total of $11,635. This is how the financial aid officer closed the gap:

College grant	$3,850
Stafford loan	1,000
Work-study program	950
Total aid:	$5,800

costs. This figure is your financial need.

HOW YOUR NEED IS MET

A financial aid package is put together to meet your child's need. This is based on eligibility for each of the various types of aid and, of course, the availability of college aid funds. Usually the package will contain two or more of the following forms of aid: grants, scholarships, loans, and campus work programs.

Each college has its own policy governing the awarding of financial aid. Every college, however, attempts to treat all students fairly, while at the same time using its aid to attract the best possible candidates for admission. Many colleges now consider the student's financial need as well as his or her academic abilities in deciding what kind of aid to award. An academically gifted student might receive mostly grants and scholarships, while another might have to rely on loans and work programs to meet the same need. Of course, all colleges must follow government regulations concerning the awarding of federal and state aid.

USEFUL HINTS

1. Fill out all the required blanks on any form you submit. Unanswered questions delay processing.
2. Make and keep copies of each document you sign.
3. Apply for a Pell grant.
4. Know what financial aid programs you have applied for and become familiar with their terms, conditions, and requirements.
5. Make sure you understand all the information you receive concerning your applications.
6. Respond promptly and fully to requests for additional information needed to process the application.
7. If you have questions about the financial aid process or the types of aid available, consult the college financial aid officer.

CHAPTER VI

Evaluating a financial aid package

N otification of a financial aid award generally arrives in your mailbox at the same time as the offer of admission. It will include details about the nature of the proposed aid and will explain how to apply for any aid not awarded directly by the college, such as a Stafford loan. You must accept or decline by a certain date. *This deadline is important!* The college may cancel the award if you ignore the deadline. If you need more time, apply for an extension.

Remember, the aid package covers only one academic year. You must reapply each year your child is in college. Family situations change, and so does aid eligibility. You may get more aid next year, or less. Grants may be replaced by loans, or vice versa. Read the fine print regarding the college's award policy in future years.

COMPARING FINANCIAL AID AWARDS

You may be considering financial aid award letters from three or four colleges. It is important that you and your child know how to evaluate these awards so that you can make a wise choice of colleges.

You and your child have chosen the colleges with care. Any

Real life, real answers.

Investment banker Harry Hough and his wife, Alice, a nurse, earned $95,662 the year before their son, Greg, went to college. A few weeks after Greg was accepted at a small private college, 40-year-old Harry lost his job. Even with a settlement from his firm, the Hough family income dropped to a projected $71,000, including Alice's $20,000 salary.

Originally, the expected parental contribution was set at $23,500, which meant that the Houghs would have to pay Greg's college expenses. Harry informed the financial aid officer of his unemployment and the contribution was adjusted downward to $12,900. Greg was assessed $800 from his summer job at a golf course and $140 from his savings.

A financial aid package was quickly assembled, including a college grant for $3,800 and a $2,000 Stafford loan to bridge the gap.

one of them would meet the criteria you set. Now it is time to become a comparison shopper.

First look at the total amounts offered. Are they sufficient to cover all the costs of your child's coming academic year? Do they include a realistic amount for the nonbilled costs: books, traveling to and from college, personal expenses, etc. See how many meals per week are covered by the dining plan. If it is less than a 21-meal plan, is there money in the total to supplement it? If the total is too low, can you make up the difference without undue hardship?

Now look at the contributions expected of you and your child. Is the parental contribution the same in all the award letters? Is the expected student contribution the same as well? You may have submitted additional family financial information to one college and not the others. If you act quickly, you may be able to obtain corresponding relief by notifying the other financial aid officers. And, if you cannot get relief from one college, will the cost difference be great enough to rule out the college, for that reason alone?

Finally, examine the components of the financial aid package. This is where you and your child must read the fine print. Practically every form of financial aid has certain strings attached, and some strings are less desirable than others.

Generally speaking, grants and scholarships are the most desirable forms of aid for the simple reason that they do not have to be paid back. But every grant and scholarship is tied to something: need, in the case of most grants; scholastic excellence and/or need, in the case of most scholarships.

Your child may lose a scholarship by failing to maintain the required grade-point average. Some grants also require the student to maintain a certain grade-point average. Remember that at a selective college, a B-plus average may not seem unreasonable, but some of the students in selective colleges had A and B averages in high school and some are now C and D students.

All grants and many scholarships are awarded on a yearly basis. Your child must requalify each year. Should your family's financial situation improve before the time comes to requalify, your child may either lose the grant or need-based scholarship or have it cut back.

Some grants, scholarships, and loans are made for one academic year only and are not renewable under any circumstances. If your child's financial aid package includes any nonrenewable aid, now is the time to think about what will replace that aid in the years to come.

If the financial aid package includes loans, make sure you understand all the terms. What is the interest rate? Can the interest rate be increased during the life of the loan? When does repayment begin? How long a period do you or your child have to repay? Can payments be suspended without penalty for, say, graduate school, illness, or military service? It is important to look beyond the first year of college. Will four years of loans create an unmanageable amount of debt?

Learn what you can about the amount of aid the college will award to your child in future years and the form it will take. Will

Real life, real answers.

Charlie Davenport is an FBI agent; his wife, Frieda, is a high school counselor who has gone back to college for a special course needed to advance her career. They have one son in college. The other, Jack, will enter in the fall. Their gross income is $80,587.

The formula used to determine parental contribution makes an allowance for Frieda as a family member in college. However, the financial aid officer at the private college Jack will attend did not agree, reasoning that her tuition is being paid by the school where she works. The financial aid officer increased the Davenports' parental contribution to $9,061. Jack's contribution was set at $1,602, most of it from his earnings as a judo instructor, the rest from his savings. This still left a gap of $6,862. The financial aid officer made up the difference with a college grant of $4,250 and a Stafford loan of $2,625.

there be a lesser percentage of grants and scholarships, even if your child has performed well academically? What grade-point average will ensure the continuation of the current aid? Can your child be sure that his or her needs will continue to be fully met?

What is the college's policy concerning outside scholarships? Will a private scholarship be used to reduce the college grant, or the self-help portion of loans and work programs, or a combination of both?

Find out if your child must accept all the financial aid offered in the financial aid package. Can he or she decline the loan or the job without losing any other part of the package?

The material you and your child were given when you applied for the various grants, scholarships, and loans will describe the exact terms of the award. For further guidance as to the long-range effect of the awards, consult the financial aid officer.

NEGOTIATING WITH THE FINANCIAL AID OFFICER

You may be disappointed with the financial aid package. Your expected contribution may seem excessive. Or you may feel there should be more grant and scholarship money and a smaller loan. What can you do about it?

First, examine the award letter carefully. Look at the estimated expense budget. Is everything included? Tuition, fees, books, room and board, personal expenses, and transportation? Are the amounts reasonable?

Second, check to see if all the aid programs you applied for have been taken into consideration. If you have been turned down, the letter should tell you why.

Finally, consider whether the family's financial condition has worsened since you applied. Lost your job? Is a divorce or separation now part of the picture? Have you incurred high medical expenses? Report any adverse changes to the financial aid officer immediately.

If your financial condition has not changed, the chance of getting your contribution reduced is slight. It is possible that a special circumstance was not explained adequately on the application—a business loss, for example, or an anticipated drop in income for the coming year. But arguments concerning your lifestyle or how inflation eats into your income will fall on deaf ears. The parental contribution is based on ability to pay, not willingness to pay. Colleges assume that educating your child is a top financial priority.

After you review the award letter, communicate your questions and any pertinent new information to the financial aid officer. If you ask for a change in your contribution, expect to furnish documentation: letters from doctors or lawyers, copies of bills, insurance company reports, for instance.

Getting angry at a financial aid officer will not help. He or she is trying to deal equitably with thousands of families and students. And no financial aid officer ever has all the resources he or she would like. Remember, too, that the college financial aid officer will have the final say over your child's aid package; there is no "higher authority" to whom you can appeal.

WHAT YOU CAN EXPECT

The financial aid officer will usually review the new information you present with professionalism and sensitivity, making the proper adjustments. At some colleges, however, funds are limited; if your problem comes up late, there may be no money available. It is possible that your expected contribution could be lowered, but there may be no increase in aid.

Perhaps your contribution seems fair, but you cannot pay the college bills when they come due. The financial aid officer may be able to help. Some colleges now have their own payment plans; others participate in plans offered by commercial lending institutions.

All information submitted to the financial aid officer is treated confidentially and used solely to determine your child's eligibility for aid. No one outside the office is given access to it. The government stipulates that the information be retained for a specified period to be available for audits. After that, your records are destroyed.

SOME HELPFUL HINTS

1. Keep copies of all materials submitted to the financial aid officer.
2. Use certified mail when submitting important documents.
3. Carefully read all communications from the financial aid office, and make sure you understand them.
4. Inform the financial aid officer immediately of any scholarships, grants, or other assistance your child will be receiving.
5. If a coach or other college official suggests that financial aid is available, check with the financial aid officer to see if the offer is valid.

CHAPTER VII

Grants and loans

THE PELL GRANT

T he Pell Grant Program, which began in 1972, was the first federal financial aid program to award money directly to students. It is now the largest student aid program that the government funds, distributing some $4 billion a year.

A Pell grant is based solely on student need, as determined by a standard formula. The annual grant to individual students currently ranges from $200 to $2,300. To those who qualify, Pell grants are a solid financial foundation to which various other kinds of loans and scholarships are often added.

Currently, nearly one out of five college freshmen receive a Pell grant. But even if you feel your child does not qualify, it is essential to apply because that is a necessary step in obtaining other forms of financial aid. State agencies and the colleges themselves expect a student to apply for a Pell grant, and it is a prerequisite for a guaranteed student loan. Most private and state sources of financial aid will not consider your child's application until he or she has been considered for a Pell grant (see Chapter V).

SUPPLEMENTAL EDUCATIONAL OPPORTUNITY GRANT (SEOG)

Another available federal grant is the Supplemental Educational Opportunity Grant (SEOG). This is a campus-based program: A participating college receives a set amount of money from the federal government and distributes it through its own financial aid office. Grant money is either paid directly to the student or credited to the student's account.

The amount of this grant depends on three factors: the student's financial need, the availability of SEOG funds at the college, and the amount of other financial aid going to the student. Pell grant recipients are given first priority in the awarding of SEOG grants.

Neither Pell grants nor SEOGs are renewed automatically. A student must reapply each year. The amount of the individual grant may vary from year to year and may not be awarded at all, depending upon the funds allocated by Congress and changes in the student's financial condition. Because each college has limited SEOG funds, it is important to apply early. The financial aid office will advise you on how and when to apply.

THE STAFFORD LOAN

To help students from middle-income families, Congress in 1965 created the Guaranteed Student Loan Program (GSLP). A partnership was formed between the government, community lenders, and private loan guarantee agencies. This program has evolved into the Stafford Loan Program, now the major source of credit for education loans. Today, more than one out of five college students has a Stafford loan.

There are many advantages to Stafford loans:

☐ Money can be borrowed without collateral or an established credit history because the government guarantees the loans against borrower default, bankruptcy, death, or disability.

☐ The interest due on the loan is paid by the government as long as the student remains in school on at least a half-time basis and makes satisfactory academic progress.

☐ After the student finishes college, there is a six-month grace period before repayment must begin.

☐ The interest rate is considerably lower than that charged on other forms of loans. In 1989, it was 8 percent, rising to 10 percent after the first four years of repayment.

☐ The student specifies the repayment time period. The limit is 10 years, although the lender may extend the time slightly to ease financial strain on the student. The monthly payment cannot be less than $50.

An origination fee is assessed when the loan is made. This fee, currently 5 percent of the total loan, helps reduce the government's cost of subsidizing the loan. The bank or lending institution may also charge an insurance premium of up to 3 percent of the principal.

If the student fails to pay back the lender, a guarantee agency pays off the loan and then attempts to collect from the student. The U.S. Department of Education reimburses the guarantee agency for the amount uncollected. This process is called reinsurance.

By providing reinsurance for Stafford loans, the guarantee agency makes them attractive to banks and other commercial lenders. There are two major guarantee agencies, the Higher Education Assistance Foundation (HEAF) and the United Student Aid Fund (USAF). Both are private, nonprofit corporations.

Some states have State Guarantee Agencies (SGAs) that serve the same purpose and operate the same way as HEAF and USAF, except that some SGAs require that the loans be insured. The annual premium varies from state to state but by law must be less than 3 percent per year of the outstanding balance.

Sometimes Stafford loans are not readily available. Banks and other commercial lenders are not required to set aside money for them or make them. A student seeking a Stafford loan is in competition with other people seeking loans for other purposes. However, many states have set up student loan agencies to make sure there is money available for Stafford loans.

Eligibility requirements for a Stafford loan

To be eligible to receive a Stafford loan, a student must:

☐ Be a United States citizen or registered alien.
☐ Be enrolled at least half-time in an approved program at a

college participating in the Department of Education's financial aid program.

☐ Make satisfactory academic progress, as determined by the college.

☐ Prove financial need.

☐ Not be in default on a federal loan nor owe a refund on a Pell or SEOG grant.

☐ Be registered, if required, with Selective Service.

☐ Sign a Statement of Educational Purpose acknowledging that the Stafford loan will be used to pay college expenses only.

Three factors determine how much money can be borrowed: the annual total and individual amounts allowed under the program; the actual cost of the college program; and the policy of the lending institution. Here are the lending limits of the Stafford program:

Type of student	Annual limit	Total limit
Freshman or sophomore	$2,625	
Junior or senior	4,000	$13,250
Graduate or professional	7,500	*54,750

*Includes any amounts borrowed as an undergraduate.

For a Stafford loan, college costs are defined as the total of tuition, books and supplies, room and board, transportation, and other related expenses. Deducted from the total is any other financial assistance being received: grants, scholarships, most veterans' benefits, including those from the GI Bill, ROTC scholarships and allowance, and campus-based Perkins loans.

The student's loan must be approved by the college, the guarantee agency, and the lending institution.

The college financial aid office reviews the application. It determines the financial need and the maximum loan amount allowable, validates the information on the application, verifies the student's academic standing, and furnishes financial information on college costs.

The guarantee agency verifies that the student has not applied for more than one loan during the college year, is not in

Real life, real answers.

George Whetstone is the music teacher in a small-town high school in Iowa. His wife, Olga, is a part-time dietitian in a local nursing home. Their oldest child, Grace, is a freshman at a private liberal arts college. The Whetstones also have a son in high school and three children in the lower grades. Their combined income is $29,873; their savings account has a balance of $1,100; and their home, minus the outstanding mortgage, is worth $35,000.

With a modest income and five children, the Whetstones' expected parental contribution to the cost of Grace's first year in college was only $305. Grace's contribution was more, $700 from her job in a fast food restaurant, another $184 from her savings account. The Whetstones' total contribution: $1,189, which left a sizable gap of $15,625.

The financial aid officer was able to put together a package for Grace consisting of grants, loans, and a job in the biology laboratory to make up the difference. Despite the amount of aid, only $3,725 of the total was made up of loans. The package consisted of:

College grant	$8,250
Pell grant	1,050
State grant	1,800
Stafford loan	2,625
Perkins loan	1,100
Work-study program	800
Total aid:	$15,625

default on a previous loan, has not exceeded the loan limit, and has all paperwork in order.

The lending institution makes sure the information on the application is complete and correct.

How to get a Stafford loan

To obtain a Stafford loan, get an application at a lending institution or the college's financial aid office. Fill out the application and send it to the financial aid office with all requested information. The financial aid office will determine your eligibility, fill out its section of the application, and send it to the lending institution. The lending institution will approve the application and submit the loan to the guarantee agency. The guarantee agency will approve the loan and notify the bank. The bank then mails a check for the amount of the loan to your college. If the loan is for more than $1,000, half the money is made available at the start of the first term, the remainder at the start of the second.

The student is responsible for paying back the loan. The lending institution must be notified upon graduation or withdrawal from college, transfer, failure to enroll for the period the loan was intended, or change of address.

THE PERKINS LOAN

The Perkins Loan Program was an outgrowth of the National Defense Student Loan Program, created by Congress in 1958 in reaction to the Soviet launching of Sputnik. This campus-based program offers loans at attractive interest rates to college students.

Eligibility for a Perkins loan depends on financial need, the availability of federal funds at the student's college, and the amount of other aid the student is receiving.

Students in degree programs at participating colleges can borrow up to $4,500 to complete the first two years of college, and another $4,500 to finish college, or $9,000 if no money was borrowed the first two years. Graduate and professional school students may borrow $18,000 less the amount of Perkins loan money borrowed as an undergraduate. The current interest rate on these loans is 5 percent.

The college receives the money to be loaned from the government or from repayments of prior recipients. The financial aid office awards Perkins loans as part of the financial aid it administers. The amount of Perkins loan money can vary from year to year, affecting the amount individual students can borrow.

Students receiving a Perkins loan sign a promissory note

PERKINS LOAN REPAYMENT SCHEDULES AT 5 PERCENT INTEREST

Amount of loan	Number of months	Monthly payment
$1,000	36	$29.27
9,000	120	95.46
12,000	120	127.28
18,000	120	190.92

agreeing to repay the loan amount with interest. Repayment begins nine months after graduation or withdrawal from college. Up to 10 years may be allowed for repayment, but monthly payments must be at least $30.

The college can demand the principal, interest, and a penalty charge if a student defaults on a Perkins loan. The college also can sue the student and ask the government to help it collect.

Repayment deferments of up to three years can be given in the case of unemployment or prolonged illness, or if the student is interning before entering a profession, or serving in the military, Peace Corps, or the VISTA or ACTION programs.

An interesting feature of a Perkins loan is that some or all of the loan repayment will be canceled under certain circumstances. These include total cancellation for a teacher working full-time with handicapped children, in schools serving low-income students, or in a Head Start program. Partial cancellation is given for service in the Peace Corps or VISTA, and in certain military specialties.

PARENT LOANS FOR UNDERGRADUATE STUDENTS (PLUS)

In 1981 Congress established the PLUS Program to supplement the Guaranteed Student Loan Program (now the Stafford Loan Program); it helps families who want to assume financial responsibility for their children's college education.

PLUS enables you to borrow as much as $4,000 a year at

an attractive interest rate. You may use the money to meet your expected family contribution.

To be eligible for a PLUS loan you must:

- ☐ Be the natural or adoptive parent or the legal guardian of a dependent student.
- ☐ Be a citizen or a permanent resident of the United States.
- ☐ Be free from default on a previous PLUS loan or any other type of student loan.
- ☐ Not owe a refund on a Pell or Supplemental Educational Opportunity grant at the school being attended by the dependent student.
- ☐ Have approval from a lender for the loan.

In addition, your child must:

- ☐ Be enrolled in a participating school.
- ☐ Be a citizen or permanent resident of the United States.
- ☐ Be free from default on any type of student loan and not owe a refund to any educational grant program.
- ☐ Be dependent on you for financial support.
- ☐ Not be eligible for additional Stafford funds.

Unlike Stafford loans, PLUS loans are not based on need. But you do have to show that there is a gap between your child's college costs and the amount of other available financial aid. As with conventional loans, you have to prove to the satisfaction of the lending institution that you have a good credit history and the resources to repay the loan. Repayment begins within 60 days after you receive the money.

PLUS loans are made for up to 10 years and carry a variable annual interest rate. Each December, the Department of Education sets the rate for the coming year by adding 3.75 percent to the previous year's average 91-day Treasury bill rate, with an upper limit of 12 percent.

Borrowers pay an insurance or guarantee fee of no more than 3 percent per year for up to five years on the declining balance on a PLUS loan. This pays a guarantee agency to insure the loan against default, bankruptcy, death, or disability.

How to apply for a PLUS loan

To apply for a PLUS loan, get an application from a lending institution or the college financial aid office. Complete the first section of the application and have your child complete the student section. Send the application to the financial aid office, which will complete the college section. Send the completed application to the lending institution. Fill out a credit application if the lending institution requests one. With credit approval, the bank will send the loan application to a guarantee agency. The proceeds of the loan are paid to you for use toward your child's college costs.

The PLUS supplemental loan program

A variation of the PLUS Program is designed to help solve the financial problems of the independent student (for information on independent student status see Chapter IV). The Supplemental Loans for Students (SLS) Program, formerly the Auxiliary Loan to Assist Students (ALAS) Program, also is referred to as the Jeffords Loan Program, for its sponsor, Congressman James Jeffords of Vermont.

To be eligible, the student must have an income of more than $4,000 a year and not be claimed on a parent's tax return. There are some exceptions. Students who will be 24 as of January 1 of the academic year, graduate students, military veterans, orphans or wards of the court, and those with legal dependents of their own other than a spouse, automatically are eligible for the program.

Students must be enrolled or accepted for admission in a participating college, make satisfactory academic progress, be a U.S. citizen or a permanent resident, not be in default on a student loan or owe a refund grant, and not have exceeded the maximum allowable loan amounts of the PLUS Program.

Finally, although the lending institution must agree to make a loan to the student, SLS loans are guaranteed to the lender by

THE SOURCES OF AID

Percentage of 1988 freshmen receiving these types of nonfamily financial aid:

Federal guaranteed student loan	21.9
Pell grant	19.8
State scholarship or grant	14.3
College work-study wages	9.8
Supplemental Educational Opportunity Grant	5.6
National Direct Student Loan	2.9
Other government aid	2.4

Source: Higher Education Research Institute, University of California, Los Angeles

the government. The lender must be satisfied, however, that the borrower has a good credit history and the ability to repay the loan.

Independent students may borrow up to $4,000 each academic year, to a total of $20,000. This is in addition to the Stafford loans, which could total another $17,250 for undergraduate education.

Full-time independent students may have the principal payments on their loan deferred. Interest payments must be made either periodically or added to the borrowed amounts and repaid after the student leaves college.

STUDENT LOAN CONSOLIDATION

Many students graduate from college with a number of student loans coming due at the same time. There is a loan consolidation available for those having loans totaling at least $5,000. Except for PLUS loans, all the loans described in this chapter are eligible for consolidation.

To be eligible, a graduate must be in the grace period or have already started to make repayment. A lending institution will pay off the existing student loans and create one new loan. The interest rate will be 9 percent or more, depending on the interest rates of the loans that are being consolidated. Depending on the amount to be repaid, the repayment period will be from 10 to 25 years.

CHAPTER VIII

Scholarships

Most parents of college-bound children share some misconceptions about scholarships. They believe, for example, that there are lots of special scholarships for youngsters who meet a particular set of criteria, scholarships that have nothing to do with need or ability.

Such scholarships do exist. The University of California has a scholarship for a Jewish orphan who wants to be an aeronautical engineer. There is a scholarship fund at North Carolina State for students named "Gatling." Harvard has scholarships for students named "Pennoyer," "Downer," and "Ellis," regardless of need. Amherst has one for a "worthy student of moderate ability who fails to win a prize or get help from any other source."

The problem is that the chances of finding such a scholarship for your child are about the same as your hitting the lottery. And the lottery will pay a lot more. Most special scholarships pay a thousand dollars or less.

There are computerized scholarship search firms that will try to match your child's special criteria with a scholarship somewhere—for a healthy fee. Such an investment is ill advised. It's easy to find out about the vast majority of scholarships. If there is a one-of-a-kind scholarship your child is eligible for, the financial aid officer at the college will be delighted to tell you about it and will consider your child for the scholarship if he or she applies for admission.

Another misconception is that a scholarship will put money in your pocket. Let's say that your parental contribution to your child's college expenses has been assessed at $4,000, and later your child is awarded a $2,000 scholarship. This won't reduce either your parental contribution or your child's contribution. The college financial aid officer will incorporate the $2,000 scholarship into your child's financial aid package if the need is being met. It may replace a loan or a work opportunity that the college had set aside for your child.

In short, a scholarship will help meet your child's college expenses, but it usually won't reduce either your parental contribution or your child's contribution.

Despite all this, scholarships are an important source of college funds and well worth pursuing. Remember that, unlike loans, scholarships do not have to be paid back, and scholarships add luster to a young graduate's resume.

There are many types of scholarships. There are scholarships awarded by a particular college, and national scholarships that can be used at any college. There are scholarships that are based on financial need, and others that do not take need into consideration.

Some scholarships are based on academic promise, others on special talent. There are athletic scholarships, scholarships sponsored by corporations, local governments, labor unions, foundations, community and religious organizations, scholarships for the handicapped and the disabled, for veterans and their dependents, for minority students. Youth organizations sponsor scholarships, as do ethnic societies. A number of scholarships available through the armed forces are treated separately in Chapter IX.

ACADEMIC SCHOLARSHIPS

There is healthy competition among colleges today for top students. Top students attract top faculty members, who attract grants and research money to build the college's reputation. Top students frequently become distinguished alumni, further enhancing the college's reputation and often contributing generously to their alma mater. Competition has led to a sharp increase in the number of college-sponsored academic scholarships.

What are the chances of your child winning an academic scholarship? To be considered, he or she should have a grade average of B or better and rank in the upper part of the class. SAT or ACT scores can be of equal importance. Your child should have scores well above the national average. Recently, the average SAT scores were 431 for verbal and 475 for math. The average ACT composite is 18.6.

It will help if your child has taken part in a range of activities in school or the community, or at church or a club. Scholarships also are available for children with special talents in such disciplines as music, art, drama, dance, or writing.

The National Merit Scholarship Program

One million students compete for these scholarships each year by taking the PSAT/NMSQT (Preliminary Scholastic Aptitude Test/National Merit Scholarship Qualifying Test). Of the 50,000 cited for high performance, 15,000 are designated semifinalists in the Merit Program, and 13,500 qualify as finalists. Some 5,800 scholarships are awarded to the top finalists each year. The total value of the scholarships is $21 million.

National Merit Scholarships. Finalists in the PSAT/NMSQT competition (taken in the junior year of high school) compete for some 1,800 nonrenewable $2,000 scholarships and some 4,200 renewable scholarships worth from $250 to $8,000 annually.

National Achievement Scholarship Program for Outstanding Negro Students. Some 4,500 black secondary high school students receive recognition each year in another part of the National Merit Scholarship Program. Of these, some 1,500 qualify as semifinalists and about 1,200 semifinalists qualify as finalists. The finalists compete for 700 Achievement Scholarships worth more than $2 million.

The National Hispanic Scholar Awards Program. Hispanics

taking the PSAT/NMSQT are eligible for the National Hispanic Scholars Program sponsored by the College Board. The program, funded by the Mellon Foundation, gives $1,500 one-year scholarships and $100 honorable mention awards to Hispanic high school seniors. Academic achievement, personal qualities, and community involvement also are considered in awarding the scholarships.

Presidential scholars

Some 120 students are selected without application from those scoring high on the SAT and ACT. Of those, 20 are chosen for achievement in the arts through participation in the Art, Recognition and Talent Search (ARTS). The Dodge Foundation gives a $1,000 scholarship to those chosen.

Harry S. Truman scholarships

This program is for students already in college. The college nominates the students in their sophomore year. They must have a B average and be in the top quarter of their class. More than 100 awards are made each year, ranging up to $6,750 per year for the student's junior and senior year, and for two years of graduate school if the program leads to a career in government.

National Honor Society scholarships

High school chapters of the National Honor Society nominate members for the 250 $1,000 scholarships awarded annually.

State academic scholarships

Many states now grant scholarships for which merit is the primary criterion. Those states in which the scholarships are generally available for study at any accredited institution in the state include Arizona, Colorado, Delaware, Florida, Georgia, Idaho, Illinois, Indiana, Iowa, Kansas, Kentucky, Louisiana, Maryland, Michigan, New Hampshire, New Jersey, New York, Ohio, North Dakota, Pennsylvania, Rhode Island, South Carolina, South Dakota, Tennessee, Virginia, and Washington.

States with similar scholarship programs for study in the state university system or a school administered by the state university system include Alaska, Georgia, Hawaii, Massachusetts, Montana, Nebraska, Nevada, New Mexico, North Carolina, Oklahoma, Texas, Washington, and Wyoming.

States that award scholarships with need as the primary criterion include Alabama, Arkansas, California, Connecticut, Minnesota, Missouri, North Carolina, Oregon, Vermont, and West Virginia. Some states award both merit and need-based scholarships.

College-sponsored academic scholarships

The largest source of academic scholarships is the colleges themselves. According to the College Board, 86 pecent of the country's four-year colleges now give more than 100,000 academic scholarships. This represents a substantial increase from 54 percent in 1974.

Some of the most prestigious colleges, such as Harvard and Amherst, don't award academic scholarships on principle. A statement by the Eastern Group of Admission Directors says: "We oppose the concept of no-need (merit) scholarships. If we awarded financial aid on the basis of merit, virtually everyone enrolled in our institutions would receive financial assistance. Students are admitted to our institutions on merit; financial aid is given only to those with demonstrated need."

Other colleges award aid on a need basis but decide who among the needy will receive college-funded grant aid on the basis of merit.

There are hidden benefits to winning an academic scholarship. Should there be need remaining after receiving the scholarship, the recipient is likely to get a better financial package, one containing more grants and fewer loans and work programs. The recipient also may receive priority on aid when resources are scarce.

It is important to know how an academic scholarship (or any private scholarship) may affect a financial aid package. If you have not demonstrated financial need and your child wins an academic scholarship, your college expenses will be reduced by the amount of the scholarship. If you have demonstrated financial need, one of three things can happen depending on the policy of the college. The college may simply reduce the amount of the college-awarded grant by the amount of the private scholarship; it may use part of the scholarship to reduce the college-awarded grant and the rest to reduce the student's loan or campus work obligations; or, in the event that demonstrated need has not been met by the college, the scholarship can be used by the family to supplement their contribution. Ask the financial aid officers at the college to which your child has applied what options, if any, you have.

Many academic scholarships awarded to first-year college students are nonrenewable. Check any scholarship your child is applying for to make sure you will not get a rude shock when the time comes to reapply.

SPECIAL TALENT SCHOLARSHIPS

If your child has an unusual talent or ability, there may be a scholarship in the offing. Some are awarded on the basis of competition, others through the recommendation of teachers, bandmasters, etc.

Art and photography

The Scholastic Art Awards include scholarships, cash awards, and other forms of financial aid. The Scholastic Photography Awards comprise a similar program.

Drama

The Thespian Society awards 30 $1,000 scholarships to students majoring in theater arts. High school chapters nominate students for the scholarships.

Leadership

The Josten Foundation makes nonrenewable $1,000 awards to outstanding high school seniors. The awards are administered by the Citizens Scholarship Foundation. The Century III Leaders Scholarship Program makes a number of awards: $11,500 to the national winner; $2,000 each to nine runners up; $1,500 each to two primary winners in each state; $500 each to two state alternates. The National Association of Secondary School Principals administers the program. The Senate Youth Program of the William Randolph Hearst Foundation awards 104 $2,000 scholarships to elected student government officials.

Science

High school seniors compete for $140,000 in Westinghouse Science Talent Search Scholarships and Awards by conducting an independent research project in science, mathematics, or engineering and submitting a report.

Writing

The Scholastic Writing Awards present scholarships and other forms of financial aid to promising writers.

Contests

There are hundreds of scholarship contests conducted annually, both general and for special talents and abilities. Some are excellent, some are little more than publicity gimmicks for the sponsoring company or organization. Before your child enters a contest, examine it carefully. Read the fine print. How many students usually enter? What are the awards actually worth? Can they be used at any accredited college? Are the awards renewable? If you cannot get satisfactory answers, ask your high school guidance counselor or the college financial aid officer.

CAREER INTEREST SCHOLARSHIPS

Colleges, associations, and companies have numerous scholarships for students interested in various fields of study. As a rule, the colleges with strong departments in a particular field offer the most scholarships in that field: Cornell for hotel management, for example, and the University of Vermont for agriculture.

The fields of study in which scholarships are available include accounting, architecture, art, education, various engineering disciplines, food management technology, culinary arts, foreign study, geology, geophysics, graphic arts, history, horticulture, journalism, librarianship, music, naval architecture, private club management, public service, real estate appraisal, special education, the travel industry, vertical flight technology, and viticulture.

SCHOLARSHIPS FOR THE HEALTH PROFESSIONS

If your child is interested in becoming a doctor, nurse, dentist, chiropractor, or veterinarian, or in pursuing any of the other health careers, there are an exceptional number of scholarships as well as other forms of student aid available.

The federal government alone spends nearly $1.5 billion annually on the training of health professionals. Some of this money goes directly to students. The programs that are geared to individual students are particularly open to students willing to practice their profession for a period of time after graduation in "shortage areas," where the quality of medical care is below the national average.

However, much of the funding that the government allocates to the colleges for their health profession programs is not passed on to the students, at least not directly. The money is used to hold down tuition to an affordable level.

ATHLETIC SCHOLARSHIPS

If your child is an outstanding athlete in a major sport, this advice isn't for you. Colleges seek out the stars and have generous scholarships for them. But if your son or daughter is a better-than-average athlete, even in a minor sport, there is financial aid available, too. Considerable financial aid is available at most colleges for students of both sexes who are good in any of a wide range of major and minor sports. But to get this aid, you and your child must work to market his or her talents.

The procedure is a simple one. Get in touch with the appropriate coaches at the colleges to which you are applying and convince them of your child's potential contribution to the team. If convinced, the coach may be able to influence both admission and financial aid officers.

Both your child's coach and high school guidance counselor can help. They usually know what schools offer what programs and what the standards are. Find out the names of the college coaches and write to them. Both academic and athletic achievements should be described in the letter. Send along appropriate clippings, statistics, and records of letters and honors won. And indicate what financial aid is needed. If the college coaches show interest, follow up by asking your high school coach to send the college coach a letter of recommendation.

CORPORATE-SPONSORED SCHOLARSHIPS

A growing number of companies offer scholarships and other forms of financial aid for the children of their employees as part of their fringe benefit program. Some 400 companies sponsor Merit Scholarships, a national program that annually makes 1,500 renewable, need-based awards. Federal employees and members of their families are eligible for Federal Employee Education and Assistance (FEEA) Fund Scholarships, 200 awards ranging from $500 to $2,500. Many major companies, including Whirlpool, Westinghouse, and Food Fair, give merit scholarships to children of their employees.

Many companies make it easier for children of employees to participate in the Stafford Student Loan Program. They set up a reserve against student loan defaults, hire a firm to administer the program, and find banks to act as lenders. Federal government employees have the opportunity to take out FEEA educational loans from $2,000 to $20,000 a year at a subsidized rate that works out to 1 percent above the prime rate.

STUDENT EMPLOYMENT AND MEMBERSHIP SCHOLARSHIPS

The job your child may be holding can sometimes result in a scholarship. After only three weeks of employment at Burger King, a young person is eligible to receive $200 every three months up to a maximum of $2,000. Does your son caddie? More than 200 former golf caddies annually receive more than $2 million in scholarships. Does he or she have a newspaper route? There are some 100 awards of $6,000 made on a competitive basis each year to carriers of newspapers that are part of the Gannett chain.

Club membership opens other scholarship possibilities. The Boy Scouts, Future Homemakers of America, and 4-H Clubs all have scholarship programs.

PARENTAL MEMBERSHIP SCHOLARSHIPS

Don't overlook your memberships and affiliations when you are looking for a scholarship for your child. Many trade groups and associations sponsor scholarships for the children of members. So do patriotic, civic, veterans', and fraternal organizations, including the Knights of Columbus, Rebekah, Beta Sigma Phi, the International Order of Job's Daughters, and the United Daughters of the Confederacy.

Children of union members may be eligible for a scholarship. Unions with scholarship programs include the Teamsters, Letter Carriers, Postal Workers, Chemical Workers, Garment Workers, Hotel and Restaurant Employees, Seafarers, Transport Workers, and Hospital and Health Care Workers.

If you or your spouse served in the military, there are scholarships available through the American Legion and other veterans' organizations.

CHURCH-SPONSORED SCHOLARSHIPS

Churches are a rich source of college scholarships and loans. For Catholics there are Pro Deo and Pro Patria scholarships and student loans available through the Knights of Columbus. Twelve $1,000 scholarships are awarded that must be used at a Catholic college.

Lutherans have several financial aid programs. The Aid Association for Lutherans (AAL) has a competitive college scholarship program offering 200 renewable and 200 nonrenewable awards annually worth from $500 to $1,750, as well as the noncompetitive AAL Lutheran Campus Scholarship Program. The Lutheran Brotherhood awards some 200 members scholarships annually, ranging up to $2,000. Nonmembers attending Lutheran colleges are eligible for some 500 awards from the brotherhood ranging in value from $800 to $1,500.

The United Presbyterians are eligible for scholarships ranging from $500 to $2,000. There also is a United Presbyterian student loan program and special minority awards. Methodists have a student loan program at 6 percent interest of up to $900 per academic year, $1,000 if the student is attending a college affiliated with the church. The church also sponsors a minority scholarship program.

The Albert Baker Fund offers a student loan program to Christian Scientists. From $1,200 to $2,000 per academic year may be borrowed at a 6 percent interest rate, repayable after graduation.

ETHNIC ASSOCIATION SCHOLARSHIPS

A number of ethnic associations sponsor college scholarships and student loan programs. These include Italian UNICO, Japanese American Citizens League, Polish Kosciuszko Foundation, Danish Brotherhood of America, Lithuanian Alliance, Polish Falcons, Greek Daughters of Penelope, the Order of AHEPA, Sons of Norway, Sons of Poland, and the Russian Brotherhood Organization.

SCHOLARSHIPS FOR MINORITIES

More and more scholarships and aid programs are being established to meet the special needs of minority students.

The Indian Fellowship Program will pay the tuition and related expenses for Indian undergraduates in business, engineering, and national resources. The Indian Health Service has similar scholarships for students in such health fields as pharmacology and nursing.

Scholarships in the health research field are available to students of any minority group through the National Institute of Health. One scholarship program prepares minority students for law school. In addition, there are many private sources of scholarships for minority students preparing for careers in certain fields, including accounting, architecture, dentistry, engineering, computer science, geoscience, social science, as well as in general studies. The scholarship directories available through secondary school guidance counselors and public libraries contain the details on these scholarships.

SCHOLARSHIPS FOR THE HANDICAPPED

There are four national programs providing scholarships to handicapped students. The Alexander Graham Bell Association for the Deaf sponsors 17 scholarships for profoundly deaf students, ranging from $500 to $1,000 per year. The American Council of the Blind awards eight scholarships that range from $1,000 to $1,500. Visually impaired students or students planning to do eye research are eligible for grants from the Ronnie Milsap Foundation. The National Association of the Deaf awards annual $1,000 scholarships to students in a field relating to either sign language or the deaf community.

SCHOLARSHIPS FOR WOMEN

The National Association of Bank Women awards scholarships to members pursuing a course leading to a career in banking or business. Bell Labs, the Society of Women Engineers, and the BPW Foundation offer scholarships to female engineering students. The Gloria Fecht Memorial Scholarship Fund and the Women's Western Golf Foundation award scholarships to promising women golfers. If your daughter is a pilot, she might receive a $4,000 award from Whirly-Girls to obtain her helicopter rating.

To learn what scholarships are available at what colleges, ask the admission officer at the college, consult the college's publications, or refer to one of the several directories of scholarships at your child's secondary school guidance office or at your local library.

CHAPTER IX

The military route to college

T he armed forces today are the single largest source of financial aid not based on need. Some $1 billion a year currently is given to qualified students, either as a payment for training or a reward for service. Male and female students with a taste for military life have a wide range of programs from which to choose.

There are the five service schools: West Point, Annapolis, and the Air Force, Coast Guard, and Merchant Marine academies. These offer free four-year courses leading to a bachelor of science degree. In addition, the Army, Navy, and Air Force offer ROTC scholarships to hundreds of colleges.

There are also special scholarship programs, including the Marine Corps Platoon Leaders Class, the Navy Nuclear Power Program, the Air Force College Senior Engineering Program, the Armed Forces Health Professions Program, and the Uniformed Services of the Health Sciences.

Some young men and women ease the financial burden of college by joining the armed forces right after high school. In the service they receive free college credit for attending military schools and learning certain skills. They may take college courses at reduced tuition rates while off duty, and the GI Bill helps pay for their education after they are discharged.

THE SERVICE ACADEMIES

The purpose of the service academies is to train career officers. Each offers a technically oriented education equal to that of the leading engineering schools in the country; however, its specialized nature may be limiting in a civilian career. All expenses are paid. Students are full-time members of the military, lead a regimented life bound by a strict code of discipline, and wear uniforms except on leave.

Candidates must be well prepared academically and meet strict medical requirements. Admission is very selective. The Naval Academy, for example, receives 14,000 applications in a typical year. Of these, 2,200 are judged to meet the scholastic, physical fitness, and medical standards. Some 1,700 are admitted, while about 1,300 decide to attend. The service academies are not large schools. All five produce a total of some 3,000 officers a year.

Graduates are obligated to serve on active duty for five years. Some special areas, such as aviation and submarine training, require an additional service commitment.

RESERVE OFFICER'S TRAINING CORPS

The major source of financial aid from the armed forces comes from the Reserve Officer's Training Corps (ROTC) programs offered by the Army, the Air Force, and the Navy (with a Marine Corps option). Young men and women in a ROTC unit wear uniforms and are under military discipline while attending ROTC classes and drills, a total of four hours a week. The rest of the time they lead a normal college life. They also spend at least one summer in training, depending on the branch of service.

The services have agreements with various colleges to "host" ROTC units on their campuses. Each unit has a commanding officer with a staff of officers and enlisted personnel to conduct military training. The Army has 314 units, the Air Force 151, and the Navy 64. In addition, there are another 1,810 cross-enrollment opportunities, under which students attend one college and participate in a ROTC program at another.

Not all students enrolled in ROTC programs are on scholar-ships. Those that are enrolled may qualify for several different kinds. The most significant is the four-year tuition scholarship. Each year some 30,000 high school seniors enter a national competition from which 5,700 are selected for scholarships (Navy, 2,200; Air Force, 2,000; and Army, 1,500).

Apart from the scholarship competition, the student must gain admission to a college with an appropriate ROTC unit, or a college with a cross-enrollment opportunity. The student also must take certain courses and, in some programs, pursue a particular course of study, usually engineering. As a safety measure, most scholarship recipients apply to several schools with ROTC units.

The four-year scholarship carries an obligation of four years of active duty, or two years of active duty after graduation and two years in the reserves, or eight years in the reserves, depending on the branch of service. A scholarship ROTC student withdrawing from the program without an acceptable reason can be ordered to active duty as an enlisted person or made to repay all the scholarship aid.

The services also award ROTC scholarships to students already enrolled in college. In fact, they award more this way than through the four-year competition. The majority of awards go to those students who voluntarily join a ROTC unit and then apply for a two- or three-year tuition grant. Non-ROTC students can apply in their sophomore year for a two-year scholarship and attend a military summer school to make up the first two years of ROTC courses. Two- or three-year scholarship recipi-ents have the same service obligation after graduation as four-year scholarship students.

Among the benefits of an ROTC scholarship are full or partial payment of tuition, tax-free monthly payments of $100, and an allowance for textbooks.

The ROTC programs are alike in many ways. There are differences, though, and these should be considered before applying.

Course of study

If the student wants to be an engineer, all of the programs are excellent, although the Air Force accepts a much higher percentage of engineers than either the Army or Navy. Conversely, liberal arts majors have a better chance of a scholarship with the Navy and Marine Corps, less with the Army, much less with the Air Force.

Vision requirements

The Air Force accepts students with less than 20/20 vision for nonflying assignments only. The Army requires vision correctable to 20/20. The Navy and Marine Corps require 20/20 vision, although a limited number of waivers are made. The Navy alone requires normal color vision for all participants.

Graduate work

For students who want to do graduate work before going on active duty, the chances are much better with the Army and Air Force than with the Navy or Marine Corps.

Time requirements

The Army and Air Force military science courses total some 16 credit hours. The only other required course is one semester of a foreign language, though sometimes language study in high school will satisfy this requirement. There is one summer training period.

Navy courses total 22 to 24 credit hours. In addition to a foreign language, Navy students take math and physics. Marine Corps students take courses in military affairs and national security policy. Both Navy and Marine Corps students have three summer training periods.

Type of commission

Navy and Marine Corps students receive regular commissions, the same as Annapolis graduates. Air Force ROTC graduates receive reserve commissions, less desirous for those planning a service career.

The Army has three types of commissions. All West Point and some ROTC graduates receive regular commissions. Some ROTC graduates receive reserve commissions. Others, who are commissioned in the National Guard or Army reserve, serve only six months of active duty after being commissioned. They fulfill the remainder of their obligations on weekends and summer vacations while serving in reserve or National Guard units near their homes.

SPECIAL PROGRAMS

Other armed forces programs are available to qualified students in certain specialized areas. Military training is taken in the summer or after graduation, not during the academic year. All of the programs are based on the same premise as the service academies and ROTC: financial aid in return for becoming an officer and serving on active duty for a specified time.

Navy Nuclear Propulsion Officer Candidate Program

Engineering and science majors interested in the nuclear Navy can receive substantial benefits from this highly selective program. It is open to sophomore and junior math, physics, chemistry, and engineering majors with high grade-point averages. Those accepted receive a $3,000 bonus and a minimum of $1,000 a month until graduation. Good grades must be maintained, and the student must graduate on schedule, but there are no military requirements until after graduation.

Graduates attend the Navy Officer Candidate School for four months, then are commissioned and obligated to five years of active duty. Training begins with nuclear power school, then six months of study at a land-based model of a shipboard propulsion system, followed by either submarine school or surface warfare school, and sea duty.

Marine Corps Platoon Leaders Class

This offers a way to receive financial aid and become a

second lieutenant without military training during the academic year. It also is the largest single source of Marine officers. Students apply anytime during the first three years of college. Freshmen and sophomores attend two six-week training sessions at Quantico, Virginia. Juniors attend one 10-week session. Students in the program receive $100 a month up to a maximum of $2,700.

Graduates enter the Marine Corps as second lieutenants. They attend The Basic School, then are turned over to the Fleet Marine Force or flight training school if selected as an aviation cadet. There is a special option for students pursuing a law degree.

The Platoon Leaders Class has a unique benefit. The time spent in the program counts toward "longevity" in determining the pay grade upon commissioning. Students signing up as freshmen enter the Marine Corps with three years of qualifying service, entitling them to $4,000 more a year than officers entering from other programs.

Armed Forces Health Professions Scholarship Program

Premed students may apply for this program in their senior year when they are accepted to medical school. The program pays tuition and fees for books, and $600 per month. On entering medical school, the student is commissioned in the Army, Navy, or Air Force, and receives basic officer training during the following summer. The student serves 45 days during subsequent summers until graduation. The military obligation after graduation from medical school is one year of service for each year of the scholarship.

The Uniformed Services University of the Health Sciences

This is a medical school in Bethesda, Maryland, at which all the students are paid as active duty military officers. Most are graduates of ROTC, a service academy, or officer candidate school. Those accepted with no prior military training are trained as officers while at the university. Graduates are required to serve seven years in the service.

Air Force College Senior Engineering Program

Each year, some 75 engineering majors in their junior or senior year are selected for this program. The students enlist as Airmen First Class and are paid about $725 per month until graduation. After attending Officer Candidate School, they serve four years in an assignment related to their engineering major.

The service first, then college

High school graduates can use military service to get a head start on college and to help pay for their education when they get there. There are two ways of obtaining educational benefits while in the Army, Air Force, Navy, Marines, or Coast Guard.

One is through "in-service" education. College credits may be earned by attending one of the many military specialty schools. There also are colleges near most military bases that enlisted personnel can attend in their off hours, paying only 25 percent of the tuition fees.

The other way is through the new GI Bill, which went into effect in 1985. The military will now put up as much as $8 for every $1 (up to $1,200) a servicemember saves for college. This adds up to a sizable amount during an enlistment.

All of the service academies and military college programs described in this chapter are open to enlisted personnel, and most have a special quota for them.

Every military base has an education office to assist personnel who want to further their education, either by attending a local college or by taking correspondence courses.

SERVICEMEMBERS OPPORTUNITY COLLEGE PROGRAM (SOC)

The services have set up flexible academic programs with a number of colleges to suit the lifestyles of servicemembers. The opportunities and administration vary somewhat from service to service.

Army

The Army Continuing Education Program comprises the Servicemembers Opportunity Colleges Associate Degree (SOCAD) and the Servicemembers Opportunity College Program (SOC). Under the two-year associate degree program, some 50 accredited colleges offer subjects in 16 academic areas. They all limit residency requirements, grant credit for military work experience, guarantee that course credit is transferable to another college in the network, and offer flexible class hours.

The servicemember pays 25 percent of the tuition cost. When transferred, he or she simply continues the program at another college, although the first college is the one that will grant the degree. SOC operates the same way but offers courses leading to a bachelor's or advanced degree.

Navy

The Navy's program is called Navy Campus. Civilian guidance counselors in this program help sailors plan their education. The 25 participating colleges are known as SOCNAV. The Navy also has a certificate/degree program similar to that of SOCNAV, except there is no residency requirement. This makes it possible to get a degree without attending class, a boon to sailors who spend months at sea. College courses are given aboard ships under another program called PACE (Program for Afloat College Education).

Air Force

The Community College of the Air Force Program offers a two-year associate degree in applied science. It requires 64 semester hours, a combination of college courses taken in off hours, on-the-job technical training, or attendance at Air Force schools. Educational counselors on the base assist enlisted personnel who wish to enroll in local colleges, arrange placement examinations, and monitor progress. Courses are given at all Air

Force bases in at least four subject areas at the bachelor's level and in two graduate disciplines.

Marine Corps

The Marine Corps has an SOC program similar to that of the Navy, and a wrinkle all its own—the Degree Completion Program for Staff Non Commissioned Officers. Sergeants who have started their college education can take up to 18 months of leave to complete their degrees. They must pay their own tuition but receive full pay and allowances during the leave period.

Coast Guard

The Coast Guard's SOC program is the most generous of them all, paying as much as 100 percent of tuition costs. It also provides special educational programs in certain job specialties. An advanced electronics technology school enables senior enlisted personnel to pursue a college degree in electronics engineering. The Physician's Assistant Program is a two-year course leading to certification and a commission as a chief warrant officer.

DEFENSE ACTIVITY FOR NON TRADITIONAL EDUCATION SUPPORT (DANTES)

For enlisted personnel who cannot attend regular classes, all five services offer a program of correspondence courses called DANTES (Defense Activity for Non Traditional Education Support). These courses are designed to help the serviceperson advance educationally, demonstrate job proficiency, and qualify for college admission. The program includes tests for earning a high school diploma and certification of job skills by professional associations. Several hundred courses and examinations are offered. They include:

☐ DANTES Subject Standard Tests (DSST). Academic and vocational examinations taken for college credit.

- [ ] College-Level Examination Program (CLEP). Up to 30 semester hours of credit can be earned in this College Board program by passing CLEP general examinations.
- [ ] Proficiency Examination Program (PEP). A credit-by-examination program similar to CLEP, sponsored by the American College Testing Program.
- [ ] Scholastic Aptitude Test (SAT) and American College Testing examination (ACT). Used primarily to qualify for college admission and for entry into officer training programs.

ON-THE-JOB-TRAINING

The American Council on Education has developed a system of evaluating the amount of college credit a former servicemember can receive for attending a technical training school, performing certain job skills, and passing a Military Occupational Specialty examination. The council publishes this information in *Guide to the Evaluation of Educational Experiences in the Armed Services*—known commonly as the "Green Book." Many libraries and all recruiting offices have the book.

THE NEW GI BILL

Under the new GI Bill, the servicemember and the government work together to build an education savings account. The military's contribution is much greater than the servicemember's. For a young man or woman serving a minimum of two years of active duty, the total amount can be considerable.

In the first year on active duty, $100 a month is deducted from the servicemember's pay and put into an "educational account." No further deductions are made after $1,200 is in the account. If the servicemember serves two years, the military contributes $7,800 to the account, for a total of $9,000. For three or more years of service, $9,600 is contributed, for a total of $10,800. If the servicemember attends college full-time after completion of active duty, the money accumulated in the account is paid out in 36 monthly installments.

The new GI Bill also allows enlisted personnel to take a leave of absence of up to two years to pursue an educational

Real life, real answers.

Billy Morris is an Army brat who decided to follow in his father's footsteps. Lieutenant Colonel Bart Morris is a career Army officer; his wife, Margo, is an English teacher. They have four children. Billy and his sister, Peggy, are in college; two other boys are in high school. The combined incomes of the father and mother total $58,079.

Bart and Margo pay a parental contribution of $5,720. A talented guitarist, Billy had saved $7,600 from the money he earned playing in a rock band in high school. The financial aid officer decided to set Billy's annual contribution at $3,300, $1,900 coming from his savings, $1,400 from his current musical earnings. The total family contribution to Billy's college expenses is $9,020.

A private college offered Billy an aid package of $8,325. It consisted of a $4,700 college grant, a $2,625 Stafford loan, and a $1,000 Perkins loan. However, after Billy accepted the aid package, he was awarded an Army ROTC scholarship. It would cover 80 percent of his tuition ($9,620), pay for his books up to $390, and give him an allowance of $100 a month during the school term. The total annual value of the scholarship: $10,910.

The financial aid officer canceled Billy's now unnecessary aid package. This still left more money than Billy needed, in effect, reducing the family contribution from $9,020 to $6,435.

program. To be eligible, a servicemember must complete the initial tour of duty and agree to extend enlistment by two years for each year of leave. Basic pay continues during the leave.

The New Army College Fund

A provision in the new GI Bill permits a service to add money to the basic benefits in order to attract recruits into areas where there are shortages of personnel. Alone among the services, the Army has done this to fill combat assignments in the infantry, field artillery, and armored divisions, and in such technical areas as electronics, air traffic control, and missile systems.

The New Army College Fund provides a bonus of up to $400 per month, depending on the specialty involved. In addition to the basic GI Bill benefits, the value to the recipient is $14,400 for four or more years of service, $12,000 for three years, and $8,000 for two years.

Benefits for Reservists

Members of the active reserve who have completed their active duty training are eligible for the new GI Bill benefits if they have enlisted for a six-year term. Students receive $140 per month for up to 36 months, for a total of $5,040. Eligible reservists do not have to make a personal contribution. All benefits are fully funded by the government.

CHAPTER X

Other ways to make college more affordable

B eyond grants, loans, and scholarships, there are a number of ways worth considering to make a college education more affordable. Which one is best depends on your son's or daughter's abilities, determination, and emotional maturity.

ADVANCED PLACEMENT

As much as a full year of college credits can be earned while still in high school, reducing college costs accordingly. The Advanced Placement Program enables good students to get a head start on college.

The program has two parts: advanced courses given in some 7,000 high schools around the country, and special examinations based on those courses given by The College Board. The examinations are graded on a scale of one to five (1, no recommendation; 2, possibly qualified; 3, qualified; 4, well qualified; 5, extremely well qualified). The grades are sent to the college the student designates. The college then awards the student credit according to its policy.

Among the subject areas tested are art, biology, calculus, chemistry, computer science, English, French, German, American government and politics, American history, European history, Latin, music, physics, and Spanish. In most subject areas, several courses are tested: conversational French and French literature, for example.

If a child's high school does not offer advanced placement courses, participation is possible through independent study.

ADVANCED STANDING PROGRAM

An alternative to advanced placement worth considering is the Advanced Standing Program. Qualified high school students may attend special summer courses at many colleges before and/or after their senior year. The classes are designed to help them prepare for the college experience, and the credits awarded can reduce the time needed to earn a degree by as much as a semester.

The Advanced Standing Program does not offer as great a cost savings as advanced placement, but the tuition cost of earning credits in summer school almost always is less than it is during the regular college year.

EXAMINATIONS FOR COLLEGE CREDIT

Your son or daughter may have acquired special knowledge in a field of learning through a hobby, a job, volunteer work, or some other experience. This can be used to gain college credits by taking a special examination. Students from bilingual families often get credit for several years of language study this way.

Educators call knowledge obtained this way "experiential learning." The important thing to remember is that it is the knowledge itself, not the experience that produced it, that is used to obtain college credit.

There are two ways for your child to obtain credit: by taking a proficiency examination, and through a process called special assessment. Some colleges allow 25 percent or more of the credits required for a degree to be earned this way. This amounts to saving a full year of college costs.

There are more than a hundred proficiency examinations in

various academic areas. Most colleges use either the College Level Examination Program (CLEP) or the Proficiency Examination Program (PEP). The College Board sponsors CLEP, and the Educational Testing Service administers the examinations that are given regularly at more than a thousand locations. The American College Testing Program sponsors and administers PEP at more than a hundred locations six times a year.

CLEP offers two types of examinations: general and specific subject. The general examinations cover English composition, mathematics, natural sciences, humanities, and social sciences. Together these represent the core of what a student should know after completing two years of college. Forty-five examinations are offered on specific subjects.

PEP tests only specific subject knowledge and the ability to apply its concepts. These tests are especially popular with older, nontraditional applicants who have gained proficiency in one or more areas before deciding to attend college.

Passing a proficiency examination does not automatically result in college credit. That is up to the college. Each school decides the examinations for which it will award credit, the acceptable score, and how much credit will be given. Find out the policy of the college before making a decision on proficiency testing.

In certain cases, a process known as special assessment is used to evaluate a student's knowledge. This can consist of an oral interview, a written examination, or the submission of a portfolio. Some colleges allow the student to choose which he or she prefers.

The policy on special assessments varies from college to college. Not all colleges offer them, but some that do not will accept for credit a special assessment a student has taken at another college. The dean of admissions at your child's college can give you additional information.

INDEPENDENT STUDY

Some colleges now offer independent study, correspondence

courses for credit at a cost well below that of equivalent classroom courses. Some students attending college take such correspondence courses during the school year and on summer vacations, often shortening their degree program by a full year. It is a good way to save money.

There are negative factors to consider, of course. The important interaction between a professor and a student is lost. It often takes more time to complete a correspondence course than it does to complete the same course in a classroom. And taking a correspondence course while in college means extra study, which means that the student's other activities and social life must give way. Not many are motivated enough to make this sacrifice.

To explore independent study, first see if the college offers correspondence courses and how many credits may be earned from them. If the college does not offer correspondence courses, it may award credits for courses taken through another college. Some colleges allow correspondence courses to make up as much as half the credits needed for a bachelor's degree. The admissions office or the dean's office will have this information.

EXTERNAL DEGREE PROGRAMS

It is possible today to earn credits sufficient for a bachelor's degree without ever setting foot in a college classroom. The problem is how to convert the credits earned in disparate ways into a degree.

The answer is an external degree program. Two states have created colleges without classrooms for the sole purpose of evaluating college credits earned from a variety of degree-granting sources. In New York, a state program called Regents College permits students to apply all credits earned from all approved sources toward an associate or a bachelor's degree. In New Jersey, the Thomas A. Edison State College offers a similar degree-granting program. Although neither Regents College nor the Edison State College has a campus or offers classes, their graduates have been accepted for graduate study in traditional universities.

A number of public and private colleges also have external degree programs. Some will grant a bachelor's degree without requiring the student to spend time on campus. Others require that 25 percent of the student's credits be earned on campus.

Although external degree programs vary in their evaluation of credit, most consider these sources:

- ☐ Courses taken at accredited colleges.
- ☐ Correspondence courses.
- ☐ Proficiency examinations.
- ☐ Courses offered by noncollege organizations—businesses, government agencies, etc.—that are recommended by the American Council on Education's Program on Noncollegiate Sponsored Instruction (PONSI).
- ☐ Military courses and programs recommended by PONSI.
- ☐ Certain professional licenses and certificates issued by public agencies.
- ☐ Special assessments of knowledge gained through life experience.

External degree programs appeal especially to the older student who has accumulated knowledge in a variety of ways after graduating from high school.

EARLY ADMISSION

If your child is an exceptional student at a school with high academic standards, he or she can apply for early admission to college, skipping the senior year of high school completely. Usually a high school diploma will be granted after completion of the freshman year of college. The financial benefit is not immediate in early admission, but it will allow your child to finish college a year sooner. Admission standards are higher for early admission; the college also takes into consideration the emotional maturity of the student. You will find information on early admission in most college catalogs.

ACCELERATED DEGREE PROGRAMS

It is possible to earn a bachelor's degree in three years through an accelerated degree program by increasing the number of courses taken each semester. The college catalog or the admissions office can supply information on the program and its requirements.

COLLEGE WORK STUDY (CWS)

The College Work Study (CWS) Program is a federally subsidized program providing needy students at participating colleges with jobs so that they can earn money to help pay for their education. The jobs usually are with public and private nonprofit organizations that operate in the public interest. The government pays the major part of the student's wages.

The government allocates funds to participating colleges to be divided among all qualified applicants. Financial need must be demonstrated, and other financial aid the student is receiving is taken into consideration. Each CWS job award carries a specific hourly wage and a total amount of money the student can earn at the job during the school year. CWS jobs must pay the student at least once a month.

The college considers the student's class schedule, health, and academic schedule in awarding CWS jobs. The CWS program is open to students at both the undergraduate and graduate levels.

The financial aid office will explain how to apply. Because CWS funds are limited, it is wise to apply early.

JUNIOR FELLOWSHIP PROGRAM

If your child ranks in the upper 10 percent academically in high school and can demonstrate financial need, he or she may qualify for one of the 5,000 fellowships awarded by this federal program.

Field of study affects the chances of winning a fellowship. About 80 percent of the positions go to students majoring in accounting, biological sciences, business administration, computer science, engineering, mathematics, and the physical sciences.

Junior fellows begin working for a federal agency upon graduating from high school, and continue working during Christmas and spring breaks and summer vacations during the college year. They can earn from $8,000 to $10,000 during their four years of college. Many junior fellows are offered jobs with the agency upon graduation.

To qualify, apply during the senior year of high school. Guidance offices usually have application information.

COOPERATIVE EDUCATION PROGRAM

There is a reasonable chance of finding an off-campus job related to your course of study through the Cooperative Education Program. More than 900 colleges and some 50,000 employers participate. There are three ways to participate in the program: by alternating semesters of being a full-time student and a full-time employee; by attending classes part-time and working between 15 and 25 hours a week; by working full-time during the day and attending classes in the evening.

Whichever method is selected, it will probably take more than four years to earn a degree. But there are some offsetting benefits. Cooperative Educational Programs can be an excellent opportunity to gain valuable experience in a chosen field. Employers view students who successfully complete such programs as strongly motivated individuals; usually graduation means a promotion. Perhaps best of all, this can be a pay-as-you-go program without a burden of debt upon graduation.

INTERNSHIPS

An internship is another way to gain practical experience while in college and sometimes earn some money in the process. Internships are of particular interest to liberal arts majors because of the limited number of cooperative jobs open to them. Each year some 1.5 million college students participate in an internship program.

The terms of an internship are negotiated individually by the student, the college, and the employer. Your child might work evenings, weekends, one day a week, or only on breaks and vacations. Usually an internship is not as attractive financially as a cooperative job or a junior fellowship, but the experience gained can be valuable. Some internships, however, offer no remuneration other than experience.

Many colleges have an active internship program and award credits for work relating to the student's major. If your child's college does not offer such a program, he or she may be able to find an internship at a nearby company. The financial aid office will have information.

CAMPUS AND OFF-CAMPUS JOBS

Employment opportunities for college students are not limited to formal programs. Every college has job opportunities for undergraduates. Your child might work in the cafeteria, for example; usually free meals are part of the compensation. Part-time jobs exist near the college and often pay more per hour than on-campus jobs. Job directories are kept by many financial aid offices.

THE DUAL SCHOOL PLAN

The cost of a college education can be reduced sharply if you attend a community or junior college near home for two years, then transfer to a four-year college for the final two years. There are 1,200 community-based colleges in the country offering programs on more than 1,500 campuses. More than half of all college freshmen in the country attend a community college.

For students who plan to earn a bachelor's degree, the community college curriculum is similar to that of any four-year college. For other students, community colleges offer training in a number of trades. Many have remedial programs in reading, writing, and mathematics for students who are not yet ready for a four-year college. Community colleges work closely with local high schools and the business community.

Once considered by some a poor substitute for a four-year college, many community colleges now offer a quality education and excellent preparation for students seeking a higher degree. The national ratio of students to faculty at community colleges is 20 to 1, a more favorable ratio than at many four-year colleges.

Another advantage of community colleges is open admissions. These schools do not require SAT tests or high grades in high school. Many students who do badly in high school attend a community college, but then transfer after two years and go on to earn a bachelor's degree. Another advantage is the transferral of credits. Almost every community college offers an academic program permitting students to transfer the credits they have earned to a four-year college. Most states have an agreement that guarantees students who graduate from community colleges with associate degrees acceptance at four-year state colleges.

Most community colleges charge between $1,000 and $1,600 per year for tuition, books, and fees. Other costs are reduced because the student lives at home and does not have to travel to class.

TUITION PAYMENT OPTIONS

To be competitive in the educational marketplace many colleges have introduced innovative ways to make paying tuition easier. The options vary from college to college, but they fall into certain broad categories. Financial aid brochures or the college's general catalog usually describe such options.

Tuition stabilization

A substantial tuition increase can play havoc with your budget. To ensure against this possibility, some colleges will guarantee not to raise your child's tuition, or only raise it a certain amount, while he or she is in attendance.

Some colleges ask you to make a deposit for each guaranteed term, or pay the full amount in advance. For most families, paying in advance means taking out a sizable loan. Some colleges and some state agencies finance such loans, often at favorable rates.

Tuition futures

Many public and private colleges allow you to pay for tuition from one to 18 years in advance at the current rate. The college has the use of your money, but you can then forget about the rising cost of tuition. While attractive, tuition futures may create problems. What happens if your child fails to meet the entrance requirements, for example, or wants to attend another college? Can the same amount of money be invested to better advantage? Carefully explore the details of a tuition futures program before deciding.

Tuition equalization

Many states sponsor plans to reduce the difference in tuition costs between public and private colleges. Private colleges use these programs to attract top students who otherwise could not afford to attend a private college.

Prepayment discounts

Many colleges now give students a tuition discount if they pay before the beginning of a semester. Others do what amounts to the same thing by giving prepaid students a payment bonus that is credited to their accounts.

Credit cards

Credit cards, such as Visa, MasterCard, and American Express, may be used to pay tuition at many colleges. The use of a credit card allows the student to take advantage of prepayment discounts or bonuses, although the high interest rates on bank cards may wipe out the savings.

Discounts

To attract good students, most colleges now offer discounts on tuition that are well worth exploring. Some of the most common types:

☐ Family plans. A tuition discount is given if more than one family member attends the college at the same time.

☐ Alumni discounts. The children of alumni sometimes qualify for a tuition discount.

☐ Recruiting discounts. Tuition discounts may be awarded if a student convinces other qualified students to attend the college.

☐ Older student discounts. Students 25 years old and over often receive tuition discounts. Colleges have found that older students usually are more dedicated to achieving academic success.

☐ Evening and weekend discounts. Many colleges offer classes in the evening or on weekends at lower tuition costs than for regular weekday classes.

☐ Campus activity discounts. Some colleges reward the contributions made to the quality of campus life by such student leaders as editors of school publications, student body presidents, and members of the campus ministry. These leaders are given tuition discounts and, in some cases, free tuition. Upper level class students who serve as resident assistants or dormitory counselors often receive free room and board.

Afterword

By buying this book you have indicated you are serious about sending your child to college. The sheer number of sources of financial aid is daunting, not to mention the procedures involved in applying for the various forms of aid. But take heart. Getting financial aid is not as difficult as it seems. Approximately $28.4 billion in student aid was awarded for the 1989–1990 school year. Indications are that more will be available in the next decade. If you apply promptly and follow the proper procedure, the chances are excellent that your child will be able to afford to go to college.

Real life, real answers.

The up-to-date library of personal financial information

How to make basic investment decisions
by Neal Ochsner

Planning for a financially secure retirement
by Jim Jenks and Brian Zevnik

How to borrow money and use credit
by Martin Weiss

How to pay for your child's college education
by Chuck Lawliss and Barry McCarty

Your will and estate planning
by Fred Tillman and Susan G. Parker

How to protect your family with insurance
by Virginia Applegarth

The easy family budget
by Jerald W. Mason

How to buy your first home
by Peter Jones

Planning for long-term health care
by Harold Evensky

Financial planning for the two-career family
by Candace E. Trunzo